THE POWER OF GOD UNVEILED

BY: Tiara L. Hawthorne

THE POWER OF GOD UNVEILED

...SO YOU SAY YOU HAVE POWER

DEDICATION

THIS BOOK IS TO DEDICATED TO MY FELLOW GODCHASERS WHO HAVE BEEN SEEKING THE FACE OF GOD AND DESIRE TO HAVE ALL THE WEAPONS NECESSARY TO BUILD THE KINGDOM OF GOD, CONTEND FOR THE FAITH, AND TEAR THE WALLS AND STRONGHOLDS OF THE ENEMY DOWN.

AFTER A LONG ROAD OF WALKING WITH THE LORD AND RECOGNIZING HIS LONG SUFFERING, FAITHFULNESS, AND LOYALTY TOWARD ME...THROUGHOUT EVERY TRIAL, AFFLICTION, AND MANY SUFFERINGS THE QUESTION COMES TO MIND, "WHAT HAVE YOU LEARNED?"

THESE ARE THE THINGS THE LORD INSPIRED ME TO WRITE AS I ALLOWED MY LIFE TO BE A LIVING TESTIMONY UNTO THE LORD. I PRAY THAT THESE ACCOUNTS MOVE YOU TO A PLACE OF FULL SURRENDER TO THE WILL AND PURPOSE OF CHRIST AND THAT IT IGNITES A PASSIONATE PURSUIT FOR HIS SPIRIT LIKE NEVER BEFORE.

INTRODUCTION

After accepting Christ as your personal Lord and Savior, you may ask the question:

"Ok, Lord Now what?" "What else do I need to do?" "These issue that brought me to you are still ever present; how do I take control?" "How do I make things happen?"

Once you surrender to the Lord there is still so much that God wants to do in your life. That is just the beginning. It's important to understand the aspects of spiritual warfare and learn how to be effective on the battlefield for Christ. The warfare doesn't just stop because you get saved. In actuality the warfare is even greater and the enemy works that much harder to eliminate you from the battlefield; to annihilate you.

You must be taught what God expects you to do and how God expects you to operate as a Christian and true believer. He has given us our weapons of warfare and the power of the Holy Ghost to aid us in our daily walk with Christ and to help us live a life filled with triumph and success.

Most of us desire the peace and joy of the Lord that we felt when we first received the gift of salvation. However, oftentimes there is a lack of teaching and direction given so that there is steady growth, understanding, and application of the Word of God even in the midst of our day to day tests and trials. Without the teaching we need to sustain us, the Word is unable to take a deep root and grow. The result then usually amounts to one needing to be saved over and over from Sunday to Sunday. We wind up loosed, just to be bound again because of spiritual warfare behind the scenes that many new converts and babes in Christ know little about.

Beyond salvation we should seek God for the indwelling of His Holy Ghost. This is very important because this is where our power comes from, and is often followed by our yoke-breaking anointing. This is the power that heals, delivers, and sets the captives free. This is what makes the demons tremble and is absolutely necessary to be victorious in battle. Without it is like being in a war without ammunition in your weapon!

As you read through this book you'll gain an understanding of what the Holy Ghost is, why you should have it, and what you should do once you receive it. Once you've finished reading, you should be empowered and motivated to pick up your weapons and fight! This main weapon being the gift of the Holy Ghost. You'll be equipped to effectively contend for the faith and put the devil to flight.

FOREWORD

"The Power of God Unveiled" is an excellent tool and resource for new converts and also serves as an awesome exhortative word for the seasoned saint! I was encouraged by the entire book but some of the points REALLY GRABBED AT MY HEART! Like the fact that our tests and trials are really things that we suffer just to bring us to an expected end.

I love the way Pastor Tiara emphasized the importance of relationship with Christ being an extension of our belief. It is so easy to see others in the Body of Christ as being anointed and very gifted; however do we really know what the anointing costs us? The passion to reach out to new believers and train them concerning different levels of the Holy Spirit's work in our lives is so evident within the pages of this book. I have personally seen the effects of some who truly become born again and possess the proof of the Holy Spirit's indwelling within their hearts by the fruit that they bear, yet the level of teaching concerning the power and gifts, callings, and anointings appear to be missing. Pastor Hawthorne takes the time to explain each aspect of the Fruit of the Spirit and the Gifts of the Spirit. The way she explains with scripture and life experiences gives the reader a more personal aspect of the subject matter.

The contents within the latter part of the book are especially important and should be read not once but periodically over again, especially for the new convert. This to me, makes this book not only an inspirational piece, but a reference book, and one that can be referred to and used throughout our walk with Christ. "The Power of God Unveiled" is a must read. I recommend this book for a lot of reasons, but mainly for the mere fact that Pastor Tiara Hawthorne teaches the principals in a way that will stir your heart to want more love, more power, and more of the Holy Spirit's work in your life! The overtone and exhortative instructions is that of a Pastor's Heart. Read this book and expect to go higher in your walk with God. Be prepared be changed. Be prepared to soar!

Minister Denise Cook-Godfrey

Worshipful Ministries http://www.worshipfulministries.com/

ENDORSEMENT

The Power of God Unveiled is a book about the Holy Spirit that believers can use as a reference supplement to live by. This is a powerful work that helps with spiritual warfare and going behind enemy lines. This book speaks to readers of all walks of life no matter the spiritual lever you're on whether you're seasoned in the Lord or you're just getting started on your Christian journey. It gives you a better, deeper understanding of the purified love of Christ and how to operate by His Spirit.

Demetrius Hawthorne, Prophet
God Chasers Ministries, Inc.

TABLE OF CONTENTS

THE IMAGE

POINT OF NO RETURN

FEAR AND INTIMIDATION

THE TEARING DOWN

THE FINISH

CHAPTER I

LET ME INTRODUCE MYSELF

WHAT IS THE HOLY GHOST?

Simply put; the Holy Ghost is the Spirit of God.

I John 5:8

> *For these are three that bear witness in heaven, the Father, the Word, and the Holy Ghost: and these three are one.*

As Jesus walked the earth teaching and performing signs, miracles, and other wonders, He also mentioned that after He left, the Holy Ghost would come also called the comforter.

The Holy Ghost is the gift of promise as stated in Acts 1:4-5

> *And being assembled together with them, commanded them that they should not depart from Jerusalem, but wait for the promise of the Father, which saith He, ye have heard of me.*

For John truly baptized with water; but ye shall be baptized with the Holy Ghost not many days hence.

The reason God had given us the promise of the Holy Ghost is so that we would have comfort in knowing that though He may not be present in the flesh, He is present with us in the Spirit and will lead and guide us in the paths which we should go.

John 14:26

> But the comforter which is the Holy Ghost, which the Father will send in my name, He shall teach you all things, and bring all things to your remembrance, whatsoever I have said unto you.

It's a great comfort in knowing that no matter where we go, the Spirit of God will go with us. Not only is His presence comforting, but it also contains His power.

Acts 1:8

> But ye shall receive power, after that the Holy Ghost is come upon you: and ye shall be witness unto me both in Jerusalem, and in all Judaea, and in Samaria, and unto the uttermost part of the earth.

Being that God is the creator of the foundations of the world and is the originator of all power, it is most definitely a privilege to not only be created in His own image, but also to be given His power and authority to trample over all principalities and spiritual wickedness in high places.

We live in a world full of spirits and demonic forces. We are not of this world, but live in it. We have been born into spiritual warfare; a war where darkness conflicts with the light. However, please understand that the war is not against flesh and blood and therefore cannot be fought with carnal weapons.

II Cor 10:4-5

> *For the weapons of our warfare are not carnal but mighty through God to the pulling down of stronghold;*

> *Casting down imaginations and every high thing that exalts itself against the knowledge of God, and bringing into captivity every thought to the obedience of Christ.*

With the power of the Holy Ghost being one of our most effective spiritual weapons against the rulers of darkness and all of our enemies, it should be at the top of the list of things we MUST have.

The Holy Ghost is also known as the Spirit of Truth. Nowadays, there are several movements (spiritual) which can sometimes be deceiving if we don't understand the difference between a spiritual movement and the divine power of God. This is where we allow the Spirit of Truth to shine through each situation.

The only way we really know the difference is because the fruits show and cannot lie. We shall know them by their fruits (Matt 7:16).

Gal 5:22-23

> *But the fruit of the Spirit is love, joy, peace, longsuffering, gentleness, goodness, faith,*

> *Meekness, temperance: against such there is no law.*

If we don't see these fruits in operation then it is counterfeit and not the divine power of the Most High God. If it's not of the Spirit of God then it's a manifestation of the works of the flesh.

Gal 5:19-21

> Now the works of the flesh are manifest, which are these; adultery, fornication, uncleanness, lasciviousness,
>
> Idolatry, witchcraft, hatred, variance, emulations, wrath, strife, seditions, heresies, envyings, murders, drunkenness, revellings, and such like: of which I tell you before, as I have told you in time past, that they which do such things shall not inherit the kingdom of God.

Early in your walk with Christ you will still see some works of the flesh. However, as you continue to grow and seek the face of God, these ungodly attributes will start to fall by the wayside. Once you receive the Spirit of Truth it will lead and guide you.

John 16:13

> Howbeit when He, the Spirit of Truth, is come, He will guide you into all truth: for He shall not speak of Himself; but whatsoever He shall hear, that shall He speak: and He will shew you things to come.

Be confident in knowing that once you have received the Spirit of promise, God will use His Spirit to teach you what it is that you should know and the things that you should do. The more you decrease, the Spirit will increase. You will begin to walk in the Spirit and be led of the Spirit.

I Cor 2:12

> *Which things also we speak, not in the words which man's wisdom teacheth, but which the Holy Ghost teacheth, comparing spiritual things with spiritual.*

Speaking of spiritual things; the spirit of God is available to all who are ready and willing to receive Him. God is no respecter of persons.

Acts 2:17-18

> *And it shall come to pass in the last days, saith God, I will pour out my Spirit upon all flesh: and your sons and daughters shall prophesy, and your young men shall see visions, and your old men shall dream dreams.*

> *And on my servants and on my handmaidens I will pour out in those days of my Spirit; and they shall prophesy:*

WHY DO I NEED THE HOLY GHOST?

First and foremost we need the Holy Ghost for the power and the authority that it carries. The Holy Ghost is necessary so that we can be on one accord with Christ. God sees all and knows all and we can do the same only by His Spirit.

I Cor 2:11

> For what man knoweth the things of a man, save the spirit of man which is in him? Even so the things of God knoweth no man, but the Spirit of God.

Once we receive the Holy Ghost, we are then able to utilize it as a powerful weapon of warfare. As stated in Ephesians 6:18; we must pray in the Spirit. When we pray in the Spirit we begin to speak in unknown (other) tongues as the Spirit of the Lord gives utterance.

When we pray in the Spirit speaking in another tongue we understand that this is our prayer language which the enemy cannot intercept. If the enemy cannot understand what we are saying than it makes it that much harder to devise a plan or create a stumbling block to hinder that which we are praying about or seeking God for.

Acts 2:4

> *And they were all filled with the Holy Ghost, and begon to speak with other tongues, as the Spirit of God gave them utterance.*

The Spirit also allows for us to have a three-way conversation with the Lord. It makes intercession for us and prays those things that may not come to our mind to pray for. Our heart tells God more things than what we can think to pray.

I Cor 2:7

> *But we speak the wisdom of God in mystery, even the hidden wisdom, which God ordained before the world unto our Glory:*

I Cor 2:10

> *But God had revealed them unto us by His Spirit. For the Spirit searcheth all things, yea the deep things of God.*

Rom 8:26

> *Likewise the Spirit also helps our infirmities: for we know not what we should pray for as we ought: but the Spirit itself maketh intercession for us with groanings which cannot be uttered.*
>
> *And He that searcheth the hearts knoweth what is the mind of the Spirit, because He maketh intercession for the saints according to the will of God.*

If you utilize the power of intercessory prayer to pray in the Spirit without the hindrances of the enemy, then more people will be healed, delivered, and set-free. Yokes will be broken and hearts will be mended…all with the power of prayer.

We need the Holy Spirit to do the works that Jesus did.

Luke 10:19

> *Behold, I give unto you power to tread on serpents and scorpions and over all the power of the enemy and nothing shall by any means hurt you.*

When I think of going forth and doing the works that Jesus did I'm reminded of Peter. Peter is one the disciples that was originally a fisherman by trade. So Jesus wanted to make him a spiritual fisherman; a fisher of souls.

Peter begins to follow Jesus as he walks the earth performing signs, miracles, and wonders. Peter is also privileged to see Jesus carried away and surrendered for crucifixion. However, things take a turn in Peter's life when he sees Jesus walking on water and He says "bid me to come." This demonstrates a transformation in Peter's mindset from being simply a follower of Christ to being a god-chasing leader. He goes from watching Christ change peoples' lives to being a life changer himself.

I believe that Peter said "bid me to come" because his heart desired no longer to be a looker-on, but he desired to do the things that Jesus did. His heart moved him to no longer be on the sidelines; watching the battle, but putting his faith to the test and being an active soldier contending for the faith himself.

There should be a difference between us and the Pharisees. The Pharisees and Scribes were full of the Word and had much knowledge but they had no understanding and no power. They lacked spiritual wisdom and understanding because there was no relationship with the Father.

John 8:19

> Then said they unto Him, where is thy father? Jesus answered, "ye neither know me, nor my father: if ye had known me, ye should have known my father also.

Relationship is so important. Your relationship with Christ is an extension of your belief. The closer you are to Christ, the more you believe; and the more you believe, the more power you have. There is power in your belief. I'll say it again, the power is in your belief. So the more time you spend with God and hearing His voice, you'll increase in power because your one-on-one relationship causes all doubt to fade away.

When Peter began walking on water, his focus was on Christ and drawing nearer. However, when Peter stopped focusing on reaching Jesus and he focused more on his surroundings and the beating of the waves, doubt crept in and as you know, Peter began to sink.

There is so much we could accomplish with the Power of the Holy Ghost. When we begin to put our faith into action and start being doers of the Word and not just hearers; then the small storms that beat upon us will be the least of our worries. Our focus should change to include the desire to spend more time spreading the Word to more people and letting them know of the power of the Holy Ghost and that it is available them.

Again, I remind you not to be like the Pharisees and Scribes. They too, were spectators. All they had was knowledge and no works. The bible reminds us that faith without works is dead (Jam 2:20). The evidence of our faith should be demonstrated through our works.

I Cor 2: 1-5

> *And I, bretheren, when I came to you, came not with excellency of speech or of wisdom, declaring unto you the testimony of God.*

> *For I determined not to know anything among you save Jesus Christ, and Him crucified.*

> *And I was with you in weakness, and in fear, and in much trembling.*

> *And my speech and my preaching was not with enticing words of man's wisdom but in demonstration of the Spirit and of power.*

> *That your faith should not stand in the wisdom of men, but in the power of God.*

When Jesus went forth with His ministry He kept things simple and we must model ourselves in the same fashion. He didn't come with excellency of speech, speaking in ways that would have people needing a dictionary just to be able to comprehend. However, He demonstrated the testimony of God in Spirit and of power. Never did I read in the Word of Christ making mention of His college degrees or telling people to call Him doctor. I also never read where Jesus needed to find a church building before He could start ministering unto the lost. I did, however, read and recognize that He demonstrated love without dissimulation and He did many works through the Spirit and power of the Holy Ghost, many of which were outside of the church.

I hate to say it but church has become so commercialized and the great majority of the Elders are unreachable and unqualified. Many who you can get in contact with don't even have the power that the position requires. They have been so consumed with acquiring great knowledge but have become less concerned about really being prepared to do the true will and work of the Lord that the position calls for.

Self-promotion should never be an option. With each new level there is a new devil. Demonic forces are assigned to carry out certain orders specifically for those of a certain calling and anointing. The last thing you should want to do is operate in a position that you weren't anointed to maintain. You subject yourself to warfare with forces that you were not meant to fight.

Please understand that the Spirit is indeed for everyone. There are no big I's and little u's. But there are different operations of the spirit which we will speak of later. Some Apostles and Pastors that I have encountered have their flock solely dependent upon them and have them under the impression that they operate under the power of the Pastor or the Apostle. Why? You must realize that God is the source and that we are so much more powerful and effective when we all have the Holy Ghost and use it as the weapon that God has designed it to be.

Yes, one will chase a thousand. But where there is unity there is strength and we could turn the world upside down when all get together in obedience and operate in our respective places as we were called to do. If we did this, demons would really be put to flight. However, we must first understand that the Spirit is not selfish. The Spirit distributes its gifts freely as it wills. We are many members of one body. There is no competition. There is plenty of work that needs to be done. As the scripture reminds us; the harvest is plentiful but the laborers are few (Matt 9:37). So let be careful not to discourage those who are zealous to the work of the Lord. We should work with those new to the faith to make sure they receive the proper teaching and that we work with them diligently to receive the indwelling of the Holy Ghost and they understand the rights and responsibilities that come with such a gift.

HOW DO I RECEIVE THE HOLY GHOST?

After you surrender your life to Christ and accept the promise of salvation, this is not the end. This is just the beginning. It is the responsibility of the Elders and Pastors to assist you with getting to the nest level spiritually. In many churches there's lots of preaching. However, new converts must get the teaching they need so that they can understand the basics of spiritual warfare and what their Christian responsibilities entail.

Time must be spent with these individuals so that they are prepared to receive the gift of the Holy Ghost. Several people I've encountered out of the Methodist or even the Baptist background in particular, happened to receive the Holy Ghost "on accident" (as it was put). There was no expectation of it and there was no responsibility training for those that had it. So therefore, the Spirit was quenched because technically it's not a part of the "doctrine". This should not be. If it is written in the Bible, then it should always be a part of the curriculum at some point in time.

There are numerous ways in which a person can receive the Holy Ghost. One of which is an "old school" way known as tarrying. Tarrying simply means to wait.

Acts 1:4

> *And being assembled together with them,*
> *commanded them that they should not depart from*
> *Jerusalem but wait for the promise of the Father,*
> *which saith He, ye have heard of me.*

Though Christ told them to wait, you still must be active in faith while you are waiting. Praising God and seeking His face are key factors. God inhabits the praises of His people, so where there is high praise, there is a much higher probability of receiving it.

Fasting and prayer is another option. Sometimes if you make known your desire to your Pastor or Sheppard they will seek God on your behalf and give you the instructions on fasting for a certain amount of days. During that time you are confirming your commitment by abstaining from certain foods (if not from all food) and seeking God on higher levels than what you would normally do. God likes to fill empty vessels. During your fast He empties you out as you breakdown flesh, leaving room only for His Spirit. 2Kings 4:6 gives us this example. Just as long as God was provided an empty vessel God continued to fill until there were no more vessels left.

There are some who do not receive the full indwelling all at once. However, they receive the Holy Spirit in fragments. This happens after you consistently begin feeding your spirit with the Word. Metaphorically speaking; with the Word symbolizing water, your cup will continue to fill as you read, apply and get an understanding of the Word. As your cup begins to overflow and run over, it is then that the Holy Ghost takes you like a flood.

Another method of receiving the Holy Ghost is by the laying on of hands. This method still has some pre-requisites which is often times a high praise environment and/or your cup running over with the Word (spiritually). Don't be discouraged if you are a new convert and your Pastor or Prophet lays hands on you but you don't receive it right away. Sometimes your mind has you request things that your heart may not necessarily be ready for (it could be other factors as well).

The question to ask yourself is "how badly do you want it?"

"What would you do to receive it?"

I Kings 19:19-20

> So he departed thence and found Elisha, the son of Shaphat; who was plowing with twelve yolk of oxen before him, and he with the twelfth.
>
> And Elijah passed by him, and cast his mantle upon him.

2 Kings 2:1

> And it came to pass, when the Lord would take up Elijah into Heaven by a whirlwind, that Elijah went with Elijah to Gilgal.
>
> And Elijah said unto Elisha, tarry here, I pray thee; for the Lord hath sent me to Bethel. And Elisha said

unto him, as the Lord liveth, and as thy soul liveth, I
will not leave thee. So they went down to Bethel.

The Spirit was so heavy upon Elijah that it made Elisha decide to bid his mother and father goodbye. It made him also want to follow Elijah wherever he went. Elisha wanted what Elijah had and was willing to leave the current life that he had in order to pursue it.

Three times that we know of Elijah told Elisha to wait and not to follow behind him. But it was the burning desire for the Spirit that kept him in that journey of passionate pursuit. He wanted it so badly that he was willing to humble himself under the leadership of Elijah so that the things Elijah did, he would be able to do also.

I believe that after watching the works of Elijah and his lifestyle, Elisha knew the importance and necessity of the Spirit of God.

2 Kings 2:9

> *And it came to pass, when they were gone over,*
> *that Elijah said unto Elisha; ask what I shall do for*
> *thee, before I be taken away from thee. And Elisha*
> *said, I pray thee, Let a double portion of thy Spirit*
> *be upon me.*

It's clear! With Elisha having seen the works being done through Elijah that Elisha knew He would be able to accomplish that and so much more with a double portion of that same Spirit. He could be a life changer and go forth not just speaking great words but in demonstration of the power with signs, miracles, and other wonders. It's one thing to hear what God can do, but it's another to see what God can do! ...and this all birthed through passionate pursuit!

RIGHTS AND RESPONSIBILITIES

There are several rights as well as responsibilities that comes with having the precious gift of the Holy Ghost. Some of you may remember going to school and receiving a syllabus which gave the course outline as well as your rights and responsibilities as a student. The same applies for those who obtain the power of the Holy Ghost. There are certain things you can expect from God and there are some things which God expects from you.

You have the right to receive the Holy Ghost and that power that come along with it. However, you have the responsibility to utilize it in decency and in order. We must be careful to use it according to the will and purpose of God.

Long before we were created, God was the originator of all power. Satan was one was anointed with the power of God to usher in praise and worship for the Most High God. Though Satan was cast out of Heaven He still had the power God had given him in the beginning because gifts are unto death and are without repentance.

It is our responsibility to use our gift for the building of the kingdom of God (not the tearing down). It is also our responsibility to operate in the Spirit and by the Spirit; not for natural or selfish gains.

Lots of ministries have taken it upon themselves to use the gifts of the Spirit to receive all sorts of gifts from church members and saints of God including monetary gifts. That's not what the Lord wanted us to use His Spirit for. Many have started out humble but have not remained that way.

We have the responsibility to let our light shine and to see to it that our good is not evil spoken of. People are always watching, even when you think no one is paying attention. Make sure you are consistently walking with clean hands and a pure heart.

You have the right as well as the responsibility to go forth and do the things that Jesus did.

Isaiah 61:1

> The Spirit of the Lord is upon me; because the Lord hath anointed me to preach good tidings to the meek; He hath sent me to bind up the broken hearted, to proclaim liberty to the captives, and the opening of the prison to them that are bound.

With the Spirit of God it is our duty to tell our brothers and sisters that the Holy Ghost is an important weapon of warfare and that they cannot survive without it.

We must also use the indwelling of the Spirit of God to go forth preaching good tidings to the meek. Most preachers you see this day in age have been "pimping" the Spirit of God. There's more to it than making money, fame, and fortune. If the poor can't receive the same Word, the same healing efforts, and deliverance, then something is wrong.

Through the Spirit of God the broken hearts should be mended. Those who have broken hearts should not be the same after their encounter with you. After being with you they should experience the untainted love of God and their hearts spiritually undergo surgery.

Those who are being held captive by the enemy because of the cares of this world should be counseled to the fact that freedom is available through His Spirit. For where the Spirit of the Lord is there is liberty (2 Cor 3:17). By His Spirit we are liberated from the law and the snares of the enemy. Know this also, whom the son sets free is truly free indeed (John 8:36).

CHAPTER II

FRUITS OF THE SPIRIT

FRUITS OF THE SPIRIT

If you have the indwelling of the Holy Spirit and are called by the name of the Lord, you should be walking by the Spirit. If you're being led by the Spirit then your fruits should show.

Galatians 5:22

The fruit of the Spirit is love, joy, peace, longsuffering, gentleness, goodness, faith, meekness, temperance: against such there is no law.

LOVE

The fruits are the characteristics and personality of the Spirit. Love is the first fruit mentioned and is the most important of all the fruits. It is also one that we see used the least.

Love should be without dissimulation (Rom 12:9). Meaning that love should not be conditional. God is love and everything that Jesus did was out of love. He died because He loved us that much! So if we love a God that we cannot see, then surely we can love our brother and sister whom we can (1John 4:20).

I John 4:7-8

> *Beloved, let us love one another: for love is of God, and every one that loveth God is born of God, and knoweth God.*
>
> *He that loveth not knoweth not God, for God is love.*

Regardless of what we see and what we feel we should love each other. It's easier said than done. Love is an action word. However, God said He wouldn't put more on us than we could bear. If God is love and we have been made in His image and likeness, then people see us, they should see the love of God in us, at all times.

Everything we do should be done in love. At no time should we be convinced to compete against each other. The enemy will try to use even the fruits of the Spirit as an open door for division and strife.

If we love God, then we should also delight to do His will and not our own. Most of us have experienced hurts whether it was a trial or tribulation but nothing beats a church hurt. We, who are the vessels of the Spirit of God and entrusted with this gift often use it to hurt others instead of loving them.

I don't know how many times I've seen ministers Lord over their members and "hold them hostage" in the church instead of walking in love. Many faithful members have come forward to their Elders to express that God has a call on their life that they are ready to accept and want to use their gifts and talents for the uplifting of the Kingdom of God.

They sit these zealous members down and tell them to wait two or three years sometimes saying they need to "humble" themselves under the ministry and one day they will be launched off on their own. Huh? I know that the gift will make room for itself but wow! Meanwhile, they are not allowed to utilize and stir up the gifts within them as God has ordained. Often this happens because of jealousy or simply because of control. Nevertheless, the love of God is not reflected.

When people aren't what we want them to be, then love seems to die. Oftentimes, it's because we know too much. I'll say it again; we know too much. We see how they live or how they may be heavy laden in sin and with this knowledge many turn their backs. This is the time when the hope should flow the most. Some of us show more love to those we don't know than to those we do. We should stand in love knowing that love covers a multitude of sins.

Your love through the blood of Christ has the power they may need to break them down and have them cry out, "What must I do to be saved?" The Word tells us that we should take hold of those weak in the faith. Your labor of love may just be the faith foundation they need to surrender and seek out the Spirit of God.

Love had the power to lay down His life and pick it up again. Love saved you and saved me. Love took out the trash in your life just like your local garbage man and it's our responsibility take out the trash in the lives of others with love and through the blood. This is our "reasonable service". It's not a pretty job. It's not a clean job. We are the gatekeepers and no one enters into the Kingdom without love.

Rom 9:37

> Nay, in all things we are more than conquerors through Him that loved us.
>
> For I am persuaded, that neither death, nor life, nor angels, nor principalities, nor powers, nor things present, nor things to come,
>
> Nor height, nor depth, nor any other creature, shall be able to separate us from the love of God which is in Christ Jesus our Lord.

The true love of Christ is patient, kind, gentle, and long suffering. We are the children of the Most High and one of the most difficult things to do is wait patiently on the Lord. Sometimes it's hard not knowing which way to go or which way to turn but we wait and trust.

He is always on time coming to the rescue. This is how He continues to show His love toward His children. Call on the name of Jesus and fall into His loving arms.

When we love it must be pure.

I Tim 1:5

> *Now the end of the commandment is charity out of a pure heart, and of a good conscience, and of faith unfeigned.*

When we go forth to do things it must be done with the purified love of Christ. If you're praying for someone it should be pure intercession. It's not by chance the things you hear about people. The Lord has allowed it so that the true saints will pray with a pure heart about the situations believing that the Lord will do it.

When we hear about job loss or someone's struggle with smoking or drinking, we pray with sincerity and pureness of heart. We don't do our works as men pleasers or with eye-service but we do it unto the Lord with pure desire for those members of the body to be healed and become more effective witnesses within the body.

Perfect, purified love casts out all fear. This means that when you go forth you're not second guessing whether what you did was right or wrong. When the Spirit moves you in an act of love there's not a lot to think about or to question. There's no doubt. There's no fear. We as children of the Most High must do what needs to be done.

Don't allow the enemy to intimidate you with fear. Don't allow people to intimidate you with fear. If God be for you, who can be against you? With His Spirit you're more than able to do what you're called to do in love.

We Christians who possess the Holy Spirit should not be the ones on the run. We should be utilizing the Holy Spirit with pureness of heart to fight effectively in spiritual warfare along with our brothers and our sisters in Christ, without wavering and without compromise.

We must operate in confidence that Jesus is with us always. Don't have a fear of falling, and we love not our lives unto the death. Keep confidence in knowing that His Spirit is leading and guiding you. It is easy for fear to creep in when the belief is not pure and there is a lack of assurance that His Spirit is what's moving you. When you're operating with a mindset to please the Lord and to be obedient, then you know the Spirit is pure and you can go forth in a good conscience and of faith unfeigned.

 Now, more than ever we must show forth the true love of Christ, not the love of the world. The true love of Christ is without dissimulation, meaning it is not conditional. It means seeing people as Christ sees them "as trees planted by the rivers of water". When Christ loves, He's looking past our faults, not wondering whether we're deserving but simply because He is our creator and we belong to Him.

So many people are hurting because they've experienced the love of the world but haven't truly experienced and recognized the love of Christ given by His blood. They need to know that no matter the situation or circumstance; no matter what their mother or father did... that Jesus was there, He is there, and He will always be there. He's willing and able to do all things. That's the kind of love they need to know!

I can remember growing up and misbehaving often. Sometimes I would skip class and sometimes I wouldn't come home. I did these things because I desired attention and love that only Christ could give. I didn't know how to love others. You must first experience and receive the true love of Christ before it can be poured upon others in your life through you.

I must admit that it was hard for me to receive it at first. I was considered a gifted and bright student with many talents but I was quiet, shy, and standoffish. I didn't particularly want to mingle or be around people. For a long time I felt unworthy of their love or attention. I knew that Jesus loved me but I couldn't understand why.

I was born the oldest of six children with a younger sister born just nineteen months later. My mother at the time was a single parent, and I must admit that I was somewhat jealous and selfish because the time that I wanted was having to be shared with someone else. Two years later my brother was born and from my perspective I was put in a place of competition. I was starved for attention and affection and I believed that it was their fault. I allowed the enemy to convince me of such foolishness and that I wasn't good enough so she had more children to try to replace me, I thought. I must admit that sometimes it was easier to believe that lie (especially when you want to use it to rationalize your own faults).

After barely graduating because of multiple absences, I started life as an adult chasing people. It wasn't conspicuous but it was subtle. On jobs I would always do extra and more hoping for recognition. In relationships I'd always hide things thinking if they didn't see all of me they couldn't get the satisfaction of hurting me. However, on the other end I'd exceed expectation with "works"...cooking, cleaning, and a decent paycheck thinking that could compensate for lack of communication which showed lack of trust and true love.

I would sometime go to church and I must admit I was compelled a few times to go to the alter call. However, my insecurities prevented me. Subconsciously I would ask myself and the Lord, "What's wrong with me?" I'd ask over and over. I would blame myself for things that went wrong whether they were my fault or not. I thought I was nothing. "Why did You make me like this?" I would ask. After my self-hatred had hit its record high, the Lord sent someone on my job to answer some of the questions I had been asking.

"There's nothing wrong with you". They reminded me that I was fearfully and wonderfully made and that I had a call on my life. I was told that the things that I had gone through and that I would later go through was to be used as a witness and testimony to others with similar experiences. It was difficult to process it all but it penetrated my heart to know that Jesus really did love me and that He chose me for a greater purpose. The chase changed at that time from being a people chaser to being a Jesus chaser. He became my best friend and I began to seek His face like never before. I wanted to know more about this love...I wanted to explore the depths that only He could reveal.

The Lord loved me so much that He gave His life for me and He poured His Spirit upon me. I didn't receive it all at once like most people have, but in fragments as I continued to praise Him and seek Him through His Word. As He poured I received a boldness to tell others of His goodness.

I needed to hear of how much He loved me and I needed it often. That's what His Word is for and this what the saints of God are supposed to do. We must pour the true love of Christ upon others.

Sometimes it can be rather easy to get distracted and become discouraged based on what the situation is right in front of you, whether it's your situation or someone else's. We walk by faith, and with love we believe that all things are possible. We pray like we've never prayed before...fervently...effectually...until something happens. We should not give up or ever assume that someone is beyond saving or that their situation is beyond the willingness for Christ to intervene. Unless He says so...all things are possible!

There was a time that I was led to visit a particular church. After the service the pastor said, "I love you". I was somewhat intrigued by such a gesture. However, at that appointed time it was necessary. The Lord knew what I needed. As saints and disciples we must be sensitive enough to recognize the unctions and the move of the Holy Spirit. Then we're not questioning what the Lord is trying to do but we're in position to assist with the pouring of His love.

Once I was fully accept His love toward me then I was able to recognize the need in others. As I grew in Christ I saw He made me over from the person I used to be. When you look at yourself and recognize that you're standing tall because of the grace, mercy, and love of Christ, then you have no doubt that He can do the same for someone else if they are just as willing.

There's no question about whether the Lord wants us or if He loves us. Yes! That's the reason He created us. However, we must have a heart to receive Him. Remember, He's a gentleman with great patience and longsuffering, but what He doesn't do is force Himself upon you. We must make the choice to love Him in return. He's there and He's with you as long as you desire Him to be.

JOY

Joy is often misconstrued as happiness. Happiness is a short-term feeling of emotion but joy is a lifetime state of being.

Romans 14:17

> *For the Kingdom of God is not meat and drink, but righteousness, peace, and joy in the Holy Ghost.*

With the filling of the Spirit there is great joy. If you are walking and operating by the Spirit then there should not be much misery. With your mind stayed on Him, the Joy will trickle from the Spirit realm to the natural.

I remember attending services at a church once after being invited and I really had an awesome time in the Lord. Not long after, there seemed to be some pressure from them for me to submit myself and be under their Apostle. Why? I already had a covering. I had been in Pastorship for only two years and they saw the anointing upon myself and the ministry God had given me. I was told that I needed to submit and be "obedient" to the Spirit of God and "humble" myself under their leadership. Then they would re-ordain me in about two years. Huh? Was that really God?

In my stupidity I continued to attend services. Though I was miserable I told myself that I loved God more than my own feelings and wanted to be obedient. I was stripped of my Pastoral title while there I was to only be called sis. I could not operate in any of my gifts, not even the prophetic. It was absolute misery.

This was not of the will and purpose of God and He wasn't the one that had me there. My joy dwindled away and it became very hard for me to get to high levels of praise. Then one day the Lord reminded me of a scripture 1Kings 13:18. There was a prophet that was given an original instruction directly from God. The instruction given was that he should not eat, then along the way another prophet came to him and state "I too, am a prophet" and it is okay for you to eat bread and drink. The key factor in that situation was that being a prophet of the Most High God his instruction came directly from God in the beginning and he should have waited to hear directly from God with a new instruction.

My mistake in that situation was that I knew the voice of God and I should have waited for a direct Word from the Lord on the matter or waited on confirmation from a trusted source before placing myself in such a position. My relationship with God was questioned and my peace was interrupted. Clearly this was not an operation of the Spirit of God.

The Lord doesn't want us to be miserable, even when we are going through trials and tests. We have joy because we go through knowing that there is no failure in Christ and He's going through with us, even when there are situations we've gotten our own selves into.

No matter the situation we ought to rejoice daily in our salvation knowing that we are a royal priesthood chosen by God. To think that centuries ago we were gentiles without privilege and now he calls us sons and daughters and has made us joint heirs. It is a privilege to know that He has counted us worthy to suffer for His sake.

Ps 16:11

> *Thou wilt shew me the path of life: in thy presence is fullness of joy; at thy right hand there are pleasures for evermore.*

Thank Jesus we have access to His Spirit! His joy should follow us wherever we go because it is given by His Spirit and therefore we're able to consistently be in His presence.

John 15:11

> *These things have I spoken unto you, that my joy might remain in you, and that your joy might be full.*

When we encounter difficult situations it is often easier to dwell on the negatives versus the positives. The enemy wants us to think negative and entertain foolish thoughts concerning the situation but the Lord wants us to have joy in His overcoming power that He has bestowed upon us.

Phil 4:8

> *Finally, brethren, whatsoever things are true, whatsoever things are honest, whatsoever things are just, whatsoever things are pure, whatsoever things are of good report; if there be any virtue, and if there be any praise, think on these things.*

The Lord desires for us to grow and strengthen in the faith so our minds should be focused on perseverance knowing that your latter will be greater. His thoughts toward us are good. He desires for us to prosper and be in good health. So when other thoughts which are contradictions cross your mind, you cast down those thoughts and vain imaginations which exalt themselves above the knowledge of Christ.

James 1:2

> My brethren, count it all joy when ye fall into diverse temptations; knowing this, that the trying of your faith worketh patience.
>
> But let patience have her perfect work, that ye may be perfect and entire, wanting nothing.

These things may seem complex but in fact we maintain simplicity in the joy of the Lord knowing that He loves us that much to continue to shape, mold, and perfect us in to the disciples He's called us to be so that we continue to have an effective witness and testimony unto the nations so that they, too, are drawn in truth and love.

PEACE

Ephesians 4: 1-3

> *I therefore the prisoner of the Lord, beseech you that ye walk worthy of the vocation wherewith you are called,*
>
> *With all lowliness and meekness, with longsuffering, forbearing one another in love;*
>
> *Endeavoring to keep the unity of the Spirit in the bond of peace.*

The Spirit of God offers peace that passes all understanding and is the total opposite of confusion. God says He is not the author of confusion. It creates havoc and unrest (1Cor14:33).

You'll find that there is no such thing as peace without the Prince of Peace who is Jesus Christ. As long as one lives with two feet in the world doing the things of the world and having the cares of the world, there will be a longing for rest and peace. The spirits of heaviness and darkness that come from living in the world won't allow you to have peace.

Peace is not a state of mind. Peace is a state of being and a way of life. Real peace only comes through having a relationship with Christ. Anything else is counterfeit and superficial. The peace that comes with having the Holy Ghost gives the assurance that everything will be fine, no matter what the situation or the circumstance. Even in the midst of a spiritual storm, the peace of God says that we have the power and the authority over situations and to do what we can do. The things that are beyond our control we give to God, standing still and seeing His salvation. Even the smallest of things that concern us we can give to God knowing that He is the author and the finisher of our faith.

You must receive the peace of God in the midst of the most unfavorable outcomes. If we quench the Spirit and we don't allow the peace of God to flow through completely, then we risk replacing what should be peace with bitterness.

King David desired to be with Bathsheba so much that he allowed for her husband Uriah to be killed in battle. After hearing of Uriah's death, he took Bathsheba as his wife. Through this union was the birth of a son. However, because David provoked the Lord with his sin, the Lord advised him that his son would die. When sickness fell upon his son, David fasted and prayed for the Lord to take back his decision, but the Lord did not. After David's son died he did not follow the normal custom of grievance, but made peace with the Lord's decision and moved on. He could have become bitter, but his relationship with the Lord would not allow for it.

I can reflect back to a time when I was a young adult. I lost my uncle suddenly. He was also my Godfather. He was my confidant. No matter what situation I was going through, he understood me and how I processed things. So when he passed away so suddenly, I was devastated. However, the Lord didn't allow bitterness to creep in. I finally made peace with the Lord's decision and not long after that I completely surrendered to Christ and I received the Holy Ghost. I cannot say with confidence that that would have happened if my uncle was still here. Once that foundation was removed, Christ became my new and only solid foundation.

For years in my life I was the "fixer". However, I soon learned that Christ was the true fixer and that He was the author and finisher of my faith. I learned to make peace with the fact that God is still in control of all things and that I needed to relinquish full authority to Him. There is nothing that can compare to the peace that Christ offers.

We must have peace knowing that Jesus is the King of kings and the Lord of lords. He is the author and the finisher of our faith. Peace and trust go hand in hand. We must trust that no matter how or where the Spirit of God leads us we are in the Lord's hands. He won't lead us in the wrong direction.

There will be times when it seems like we are on the mountain top. There will be other times when it seems like we are in the valley low, but whether we are abased or whether we abound, we should be comforted with the peace given by the Holy Spirit knowing that God is able to do all things and He who has begun a good work in you will perform it until the day of Christ Jesus. Jesus doesn't do things "just because". He does things according to plan, hoping to perfect you on the potter's wheel hoping to make us more and more like Him.

Sometimes things will look completely contradictory to what the Lord says. However, we don't go by what the natural eye says.

Sometimes the natural eye will lie. The natural eye shows us boundaries when the Spirit of God proclaims liberty. We go in peace knowing that the Holy Spirit is the Spirit of Truth and cannot lie.

Jesus is the writer of your story. He's a great writer and when He's the author, we have testimony after testimony but the story doesn't end because He's the author of eternal life. So then we grow from faith to faith and glory to glory knowing that faith comes by hearing and hearing by the Word. There we have so much peace!

LONGSUFFERING

2 COR 6:3-6

> *Giving no offense in anything that the ministry be not blamed.*
>
> *But in all things approving ourselves as the ministers of God, in much patience, in afflictions, in necessities, in distresses,*
>
> *In stripes, in imprisonments, in tumults, in labors, in watchings, in fastings;*
>
> *By pureness, by knowledge, by longsuffering, by kindness, by the Holy Ghost, by love unfeigned....*

The Spirit of God is not hasty but is patient and longsuffering. These days many of us desire the benefits of righteousness and faithfulness without *BEING* righteous and faithful. We desire "microwave" results without doing any real work. We all have a cross to bear and there are no shortcuts.

Mark 14:27

> *And whosoever doth not bear his cross, and come after me, cannot be my disciple.*

The tests and trials that we suffer as Christians are to bring us to an expected end. They are to build up our most Holy faith. The suffering assists with building our relationship with Christ, increases our anointing, and gives us true understanding of what warfare is all about.

It is easy to seemingly get jealous of a brother or sister in Christ when you see them highly anointed and gifted. However, you better believe long suffering and death of the flesh is what got them there. Anything worth having is worth fighting for. So we should endure hardship as good soldiers of Christ (2Tim2:3).

The thing we need to be conscious of is that we are truly suffering for Christ. If you are not suffering for Christ then your suffering indeed is in vain. Be sure your sacrifices are for Christ and for the sake of walking in Holiness. Some of us suffer but it's because we have not truly surrendered to the will and purpose of Christ. Some of us have said with our mouths that we are Christians but our lifestyle tells another story.

All of us want to hear of the rewards for being a Christian and a child of the Most High God but the Lord will test you to see how committed you really are. Are you really willing to give up your old way of life and focus on the things above? Are you really willing to forsake your mother, father, and family to walk this new way of life? Will you sacrifice the cares of the world and the desires of the flesh?

Deut 32:17

> *They sacrificed unto devils, not to God; to gods whom they knew not, to new gods that came newly up, whom your fathers feared not.*

1Cor 10:20

> *But I say, that the things which the Gentiles*
> *sacrifice, they sacrifice to devils, and not God: and I*
> *would not that ye should fellowship with devils.*

The fact is that by nature no one wants to suffer. It seems like as soon as we become Christians, we become so easily offended; more so now, than when we were in the world. It's almost as if we try to find reasons why we should be offended. It's a funny thing knowing that the majority of the offenses originate from within the Christian sector (friendly fire).

We must learn to be accountable to one another and to take rebuke knowing that it is a part of the road to righteousness.

I Corinthians 6:7

> *Now therefore there is utterly a fault among you,*
> *because ye go to the law one with another. Why do*
> *ye not rather take wrong? Why do ye not rather*
> *suffer yourselves to be defrauded?*

There is great warfare from day to day. The last thing we need is to be side tracked or distracted by foolish small battles among each other. Our power is greatly needed against the true enemy who desires to wear out the saints. If he can turn us against each other, then we won't have the strength to master the real warfare and experience the victory that God intended.

We must choose our battles wisely, being led of the Spirit. How can we be effective in battle if we have the wrong focus? How can we be victorious if we are not taking the warfare seriously? We must be mature in Christ and carry our cross. We cannot allow the small things which have nothing to do with our mission, deter us. Division is not from the Lord but of the enemy. A house divided cannot stand and when it's successful it leaves an open door for the enemy to divide as well as conquer.

Acts 5:41

> *And they departed from the presence of the council, rejoicing that they were counted worthy to suffer shame for His name.*

When I first answered the call on my life for ministry, it seemed as if the trials and tribulations increased to the tenth power. I said "yes" to the Lord because of the Love and passion I had for Him. But I was naïve to all of what would be required of me in order to effectively function in my spiritual roles and duties. However, it wasn't long before I discovered some of the many mysteries of this ancient spiritual battleground.

Oftentimes, many cry out because of their struggles with people, brethren, or even finances and the like. However, overseas, and all across the world many are faced with death because of their relationship with Jesus Christ. The question has often been asked, "Will you die for Him?" and the answer is, "yes." In reality the majority can't even live for Him, let alone die for Him. If you say you will die for Him then why not start by letting your flesh die and putting your own will under subjection? Longsuffering is a major contributor to death of the flesh but just like with anyone struggling to live or fighting for their life, it's a "by any means necessary" situation and the same goes for the flesh. The flesh will try to survive "by any means necessary", making it much harder to walk and operate in the Spirit.

Romans 7:19-21

> For the good that I would I do not: But the evil which I would not, that I do.
>
> Now if I do that I would not, it is no more I that do it, but sin that dwelleth in me.
>
> I find then a law, that, when I would do good, evil is present with me.

Let's walk confident knowing that we are truly walking and suffering for righteousness sake. There is a way that seems right to a man but the end is destruction. Beyond the knowing is the doing.

I Peter 3:14; 17

> But and if ye suffer for righteousness' sake, happy are ye: and be not afraid of their terror, neither be troubled;
>
> For it is better, if the will of God be so, that ye suffer for well doing, than for evil doing.

Don't suffer as a murderer or a busy body. Be sure that you're not longsuffering because you cannot control your mouth or keep your tongue under subjection. Don't put yourself in a suffering way simply because you keep up a whole lot of mess!

On numerous occasions the Lord shared with me that there have been some who had petitioned for my demise. What!!!? Yes; my own people! Those claiming to be Christians; they wanted me dead! They used their power to stir up chaos and confusion, supposing that they are helping themselves. In actuality they are harming others and shall reap the whirlwind; falling in their own traps that they've set for others.

I Timothy 1:15-16

> *This is the faithful saying, and worthy of all acceptation, that Christ Jesus came into the world to save sinners; of whom I am chief.*
>
> *Howbeit, for this cause I obtained mercy, that in me first Jesus Christ might shew forth all long suffering, for a pattern to them which should hereafter believe on Him to life everlasting.*

Sometimes we can get so caught up with day to day activities in our lives that we tend to forget about long suffering with Christ. Some may think of long suffering as something you do when there is a crisis. However, long suffering is a way of life and part of our walk of faith.

Christ long suffers with us every day through our stubborn, meticulous ways of being. It is easy to get offended by situations or circumstances, even experiences we face. However, we go through it knowing that we are suffering for Christ's sake.

There was a period in my life where the Lord blessed me to have a child. Afterword I wanted to go back to work but the Lord had other plans for me to stay at home. This is something that was difficult to fathom. I was nursing my daughter at the time and she refused to take a bottle. I thought I would be slick and go back to work anyway, but how could I if she wouldn't take a bottle? I thought.

Some may enjoy being a stay at home parent but I must admit that it was something that I needed to work on. Initially I had a bad attitude inwardly about it. I went through cycles of feeling useless and worthless. I felt like my talents were being wasted. Then the Spirit of the Lord took reign over my life regarding the long suffering and I recognized how patient the Lord had been toward me regarding the matter. I had been spoiled and selfish and my daughter needed me. When this revelation was made known to me I began to embrace my new role and though it seemed like I wasn't accomplishing much naturally, I was accomplishing a great deal spiritually. I grew leaps and bounds and began to walk in the call God had on my life.

Each day is a day of long suffering and faith. The Lord is the writer of the story of our lives ad if we already know what's going to happen then we're no longer walking by faith. We must trust the Lord as being the author and finisher of our faith and believe that with each new day He is going to write something great and things will work together for our good.

Jesus has come and set the standard and a pattern for us to walk after. If He could do it, then we can do it also with the helper we know to be the Spirit. So let it reign!

GENTLENESS

1 Thess 2:7-8

> *But we were gentle among you even as a nurse cherisheth her children:*

> *So being affectionately desirous of you, we were willing to have imparted unto you, not the gospel of God only, but also our own souls, because you were dear unto us.*

Maybe you've heard the saying that the Lord God is a gentlemen; He will only come in so long as He is invited. This saying is true. Jesus is patient and longsuffering desiring for all to come to the knowledge of the truth because He is the Truth. However, He is a God of free will and choice. At no time will God force you to choose Him or His instruction. He leaves us with the option.

There have been times that I have encountered wives who have tried to force their husbands to change or surrender right away without having patience and using gentleness. Even the greatest harvest requires seeds sown and sown, watered and watered, and fertilized before showing itself fruitful.

Keep in mind that the same Jesus that saved you is the same Jesus that can save them. However, some ground takes more tilling than other ground. This is one reason why God reminds us that there are different operations of the Spirit.

As a Pastor who is called to operate as a "Jeremiah Ministry", meaning that I'm considered the "weeping" pastor and my husband, the "weeping" Prophet, I must admit that it was somewhat hard to find balance in the beginning. Being a ministry called to speak of God's judgments and carrying a sense of urgency in our message, it was rather frustrating to relay such a Word with gentleness of the Spirit. In order to be effective in gentleness, you must first have that desire for it. You should desire to please God and operate in His love. With those desires the gentleness becomes manifest as you're carrying out God's will and purpose. With the true love of God, and having a heart of worship, the gentleness of Spirit becomes a natural thing as you grow.

Our role as the vessel is to be obedient and sow. One may sow seeds of life, others may water, but only God grants the increase. The Holy Spirit doesn't beat people up with the Word. The Spirit is gentle, working and working on your heart creating a hunger that only God can fill in due season.

The relationship between David and Saul shows us the perfect example of this. God is no respecter of persons and even though this story originates in the Old Testament, it is very relevant. No matter how many times David was presented with the opportunity to annihilate Saul and handle him kike a true enemy, David loved the Lord and respected the anointing placed on Saul's life. He handled Saul with gentleness and didn't allow emotions to dictate his actions. He desired peace and pursued it. Regardless of those people on the outside of the situations instigating and manipulating situations, pitting Saul against David.

I was humbled by The Lord in a personal situation in this very area of gentleness. At The age of twelve my son accepted the Christ as his personal Lord and Savior. He also stated at that time that he desired to receive the gift of the Holy Ghost. The only problem was his intent and reasoning. There were other young adults and teens at church who were saved and had the Holy Ghost with the evidence of speaking in tongues. He was godly jealous and wanted what they had, not because he desired a relationship but because he didn't want to feel "left out."

This thing bothered me to the point of obsession. I knew his intent was amiss. I was the pastor and my motto that I declared was that I was seeking the face of God like never before. I had had enough encounters with those who made mockery of the church and didn't take Christ seriously. My emotions within me were stirred up knowing that his desire wasn't of a genuine nature. All that I taught him had been going in one ear and out of the other. I couldn't be gentle and I didn't want to! He represented me, but what he portrayed to others was nothing like me. I had zero tolerance of game playing. Every time I saw his fake praise and worship or heard his showy prayers I wanted to react carnally.

From the outside looking in one may say, "Have a little more patience." However, I believe it takes just as much time and effort to be fake as it does to be real and authentic. Nevertheless, the Lord continued to remind me that I must give the Word and leave it there. Let God give the increase. The whole while I was thinking, "I didn't pressure him to do anything. That was his choice. Why wouldn't he just do things the right way?"

"Folks want the prize without paying the price", I thought. I just couldn't accept it. I considered myself to be an excellent teacher with power and anointing, but this boy was taking me places spiritually that I just didn't want to experience. I couldn't stand him. I found it hard to even look at him. At the tender age of fifteen, there was still no ounce of desire for a relationship, just a whole lot of fronting. I couldn't take it anymore. I had other members with similar issues as it was (you'll hear of it in later chapters), but this was my child! I cried out to God over and over to release me from this mess. I mean he ran through the church during praise and worship as if he was moved by the Holy Ghost. He jumped up and down and tried speaking in tongues. I thought I would go to jail for laying hands on this kid. My anger kindled so great…all because he wanted to carry this façade. I begged the Lord, "Please deliver me. I want him to stay at home. I don't even want to allow him in the service. Lord, please, I cried. There are so many other people that I can find who will receive. He was an embarrassment. The Lord simply stated that His grace was sufficient and that I had to treat him like I would any other member and naturally I wouldn't tell anyone that they couldn't come and here the Word. The Lord also reminded me that He doesn't give assignments "just because". All things work together for their good and will come to their expected end.

James 1:3

> *Knowing this, that the trying of your faith worketh patience.*

I had the wrong focus. My focus was on the work that I was doing, when it should have been on being obedient and delighting to do the will of the Lord. I shouldn't have been focused on the Lord's job; the increase.

Over time I made my son feel completely uncomfortable. I told him that if he didn't want to be real and seek the face of God, then he needed to find another place to live. I said I wasn't going to be dealing with his spirits he was bringing home. I put oil on everyone's head every night. I told him that the next time he ran through the church like he had the Holy Ghost I was going to choke the life out of him. I made him read every book there was on hell. Through all of this, his heart didn't budge.

This goes to show that nothing is done on our time or by our own power. The Lord ordains times and seasons for all things and I couldn't "make" anything happen on my own. I wanted my son to be a God Chaser. I wanted his seek to be authentic.

We can have the right desires but go about implementing things in the wrong way. I wanted my son to have a relationship with Christ because it was his own desire and not because he wanted to appease me or fit in with the other youth members. He was at the age of accountability and it was his own decision to make.

Sometimes God will provoke a godly jealousy ultimately resulting in a lasting relationship and an eternal reward on High.

Rom 10:19

> But I say, did not Israel know? First Moses saith, I will provoke you to jealousy by them that are no people, and by a foolish nation I will anger you.

Through these difficult tests of obedience with my son, I myself, was provoked to seek God the more, and praise Him the more. I learned temperance, patience, and longsuffering even through my anger. I also learned that we cannot override the Lord's process, but we can elevate above our earthly situations and cast our cares on the things above.

PSALMS 18:35

> Thou hast also given me the shield of thy salvation: and thy right hand hath holden me up, and thy gentleness hath made me great.

The Lord is as gentle as a Sheppard should be. He desires for us to be wise and yet gentle as doves. The gentleness is what draws us and nurtures us. We must be gentle with others just as the Lord has been gentle. Sometimes we're not as gentle and patient with others as we desire the Lord to be with us. The word mingled with the Spirit breaks down the flesh and the dirt that comes along with it. Some people have gone through things and require more cleansing than others. Our love for them shouldn't change but we should pour even the more.

Jesus is that still small voice reminding us of His love the He won't leave us or forsake us and we should be inclined to do the same. We condescend to the lowly estate and recognize that Jesus has set the standard for us to live by. He humbled himself and condescended so that through His ministry, we too, might become joint heirs with Him.

As a Pastor I was often perplexed by the rejection of many. I knew they weren't rejecting me but I still took it personally within myself. I would see the hurts and sufferings of many and I could even feel it within my spirit. I knew what potential they had because all things are possible through Christ. Their mouths said they wanted Christ but their actions showed something different. I loved them. I wanted the best for them, but I wanted them to want Christ more. I didn't want them to simply tell me philosophies or words they thought I wanted to hear. I wanted to ignite a passionate pursuit and sometimes this made me want to scream to the roof tops. They said they wanted to surrender. They said they wanted more. I told them what I was led to tell them but they didn't do it. Sometimes the Lord reveals things by His Spirit and it is so clear and it makes us want to go beyond gentleness but it is then that we know it is not the spirit of gentleness but our own fleshly selves. Regardless of what we know even if it is right, we must recognize and represent the Spirit of God as the gentleman that He is. He is persistent, but He is still gentle. We may say things over and over because "faith comes by hearing". However, we must still do it in love with gentleness.

Sometimes we want people to understand us. We want them to be on the same spiritual level. We want them to seek like we seek. We want them to go with us the heights and depths that we go. But we must not confuse the Lord's will with our own. Some people take longer to come around and what I've learned is there is a difference between encouragement and increase. Meaning that we can motivate and encourage others to go the extra mile but then you can be in the Lord's way if you begin pushing to see the increase that only God can give. We plant, and others may water, but we must allow the Lord to grant the increase. Anything beyond sincere motivation and encouragement is more like manipulation and control which are not fruits of the spirit and are far from being gentle. Love in its purest form is gentle and rarely misunderstood. As much as we love our brethren we must do our job only and let the Spirit of God do His.

Chastening

What about Chastening?

Hebrews 12:6-7 & 11

> *For whom the Lord loveth He chasteneth, and scourgeth every son whom He receiveth.*
>
> *If ye endure chastening, God dealeth with you as with sons; for what son is He whom the Father chasteneth not?*
>
> *Now no chastening for the present seemeth to be joyous, but grievous: nevertheless afterward it yieldeth the peaceable fruit of righteousness unto them which are exercised thereby.*

Though the Lord chastens His children, He does it in love and gentleness of the Holy Spirit. This is not to say that the Lord is not stern and straight forward. Christ doesn't always come in a whisper especially when He's chastening. However, He's not a bully. There is a difference. We may hear the sternness of His voice in the Spirit but He doesn't come in a way that's conceived as "backbiting" or name calling and things of the sort. He doesn't use your past against you to hurt you or bring things up that you've already been forgiven for (however, reflecting on His mercy is altogether different). His chastening is considered edifying, not "punishment". He may send an angel in the wee hours of the night and have you praise all night until you have to leave for work. You lose some sleep but your spirit is edified and the Lord is glorified. I saw my husband chastened once for about four hours it seemed and he was marching in the Spirit non-stop like a soldier. He was edified and the Lord was glorified. In these situations it seemed like it wouldn't come to an end. Nevertheless, it brought forth the fruits of righteousness as the Lord designed. The spirit man is strengthened and testimonies established for the edification of the saints (the body of Christ). All the while these things are still done in the spirit of gentleness, and holiness with love purified.

I Corinthians 9:22

> To the weak became I as weak, that I might gain the weak: I am made all things to all men that I might by all means save some.

In all of our doings, our comings, our goings, we are made all things that we might by all means save some! This means that we don't give up but we become more fervent in spirit that we may come before the Lord saying that we utilized all means given to us distributed through His Spirit. Then we stand still and see the salvation of the Lord.

Though things may get tough and in the natural it may be seeming like we are going nowhere. However, in the Spirit you've gone leaps and bounds and gained so much lead way. We unify in the Spirit and stir up the gifts and talents that the Lord has given us by the Spirit. Be sure the means we use are in love and gentleness of the Spirit and that you stay true to the ministry wherein you were called for all of us first is the ministry of reconciliation. Don't get weary in well doing. Don't get faint. Give the Word and when it seems like heaviness is upon you, use the garment of praise to elevate above the circumstance and turn weights and burdens over to the Lord who has already paid the price.

FAITH

Hebrews 11:1

> *Now Faith is the substance of things hoped for and the evidence of things not seen.*

It is only by Faith that we acquire the great gift of the Holy Ghost. Jesus is faith and with Him all things are possible. Activation of faith has us move and operate according to the will and purpose of Christ.

Rom 1:17

> *For therein is the righteousness of God revealed from faith to faith: as it is written, the just shall live by faith.*

If there be any faith then there will be evidence to reflect such faith. Yours works of signs, miracles, and wonders is evidence of the Holy Ghost within you. If these works don't follow then you may want to do a faith check. You can't even get a prayer through without the faith and belief that it will come to pass.

How do you get more faith?

Faith beyond the initial measure given by God is built over time with passionate pursuit of a relationship with Christ. Faith comes by hearing what Jesus has done in the life of others (testimony). Faith is also built by going through trials and tribulations of life solely with the dependence on your Savior to get you through.

Oftentimes, I prayed passionate prayers to Christ stating that I desired more faith and power to believe and operate in Him. However, when the Lord began to initiate the faith building tests in my life I often ran to man to bail me out in the midst of what God was trying to establish on my behalf. Needless to say, I failed because of my lack of trust and total dependence on God. Of course, each person's situations are different. But my problem was my inability to wait on God without the assistance of man.

I'm the one that initiated the prayers and they were passionate, heartfelt prayers of hunger. The issue at hand was my faith. Faith was a spiritual problem that had no natural solution. It needed to be handled spiritually. Every time He tested me with circumstances, I went to someone else just before He would intervene on my behalf. Because of the lack of trust I found myself repeating things until I truly waited on God.

There was one situation where I had fallen short of the finances needed to pay the monthly mortgage payment. Being the over analytical person that I am; I analyzed the entire situation. Since I was self-employed, I looked over the expenditures and asked God over and over again "where could I have trimmed costs." I got nothing. I had meetings and analyzed the sales and marketing strategies. Could I have done anymore to maximize outside advertising and marketing? No. Then I went to the Lord and begged and pleaded. "Please God, provide the funds for the mortgage. I don't know how I fell short but I'm trying to rebuild my credit and I don't want to get overwhelmed with late payments and the fees associated. Please Lord, help me!" Nothing came through. Discomfort set in after much prayer, fasting, and analyzing. Then I reasoned within myself and said "I have not, because I ask not." Soon after, I went down the line calling family and friends asking for financial assistance (many family members who didn't particularly care for me and who would be thrilled to see me in need). It hurt me inside to have to do it. With each call I grew more and more upset with the Lord. I said, "I can't believe it's come to this, Lord. You said you would provide my needs according to your riches in glory. This same subject you have me preach about seemingly doesn't apply to me. How can you have me preach something to others that you won't even do for me?"

Then the Holy Ghost nudged my conscience and said "this is your exercise, soldier. You requested more faith, yet when placed in a situation, you refused to wait on God to provide. You took it upon yourself to "help" God by calling others into YOUR exercise. Soldier, there are no short cuts and you must know and understand that God is not a half-way God. God is an all or nothing God." All-the-way operations of the Spirit require all-the-way surrender of the vessel.

Don't allow confusion to set in when it comes to the Word of God. There is a difference between being uncomfortable (out of your comfort zone) because God is making you over and being uncomfortable because the Holy Ghost in you is telling you that you're going in the wrong direction. When in doubt, ask the Lord to make His will clear. Then give God time to respond. Stay on your face until it is clear what to do. Then stand still and see the salvation of the Lord.

When praying about situations make your prayers detailed and specific so that when you're presented with trials or situations you'll know who to involve and who to eliminate. Keep in mind that God wants us to be humble. However, there is a difference humility and humiliation. If you've been delivered from Egypt I believe God will not require you to go back to Pharaoh for support (FYI). So don't allow the enemy to have you rationalize the need to do so.

Rom 10:17

> *So then faith cometh by hearing, and hearing by the Word of God.*

1 Cor 3:10-13

> *According to the grace of God which is given unto me, as a wise masterbuilder, I have laid the foundation, and another buildeth thereon. But let every man take heed how he buildeth there upon.*

> *For other foundation can no man lay than that is laid, which is Jesus Christ.*

> *Now if any man build upon this foundation gold, silver, precious stones, wood hay, stubble;*

Every man's work shall be made manifest: for the day shall declare it because it shall be revealed by fire; and the fire shall try every man's work of what sort it is.

We must have our own foundation and that foundation must but be solid. Many people have been going too long on the foundation of others and not having established their own. I understand that faith comes by hearing and hearing by the Word (Rom 10:17), but the hearing should stimulate enough faith to trigger your own seek for the face of God so that you might find him and establish your own relationship.

Rom 15:1

We then that are strong ought to bear the infirmities of the weak, and not to please ourselves.

Though some may be weak on occasion and must utilize our foundation from time to time, it should only be temporary. Jesus gives us all a measure of faith and lays the foundation for us to build upon. He is the master builder but the only way to have a solid, stable foundation is with your own relationship. What you know about Him and what you heard can only go so far. You must experience him for yourself. You need that God encounter!

There was a person that the Lord commissioned me to sow into. I take my call very seriously and strive for obedience. Nevertheless, I sowed all I could possibly sow with that person (it seemed). I prayed and I fasted. I taught this way, and then I taught that way, but to no avail. There was just no comprehension coming to them. Every time this person would go through a trial or test they would fail and begin backsliding. When I asked simple questions as to how they could allow themselves to fall, they would make all sorts of excuses. They stated that they needed me there to pray with them and to initiate praise and worship. They were extremely dependent on me and were functioning on my foundation. When faced with their own trials and given the opportunity to know God as their deliverer they bailed and gave up. This person did things out of religion and not out of passion for the heart of God. They had become used to doing things simply to be obedient to their "Pastor", but not to learn of the Lord. This makes for an unstable foundation and it will never withstand any spiritual weather or turbulence. You must have the right intentions and a desire to please God.

This situation continued to repeat itself for a matter years. I grew frustrated some of the time but then realized that I had to trust that the Lord knew what He was doing. Who was I to counsel the Lord or tell the potter what to make?

Rom 14:1

> Him that is weak in the faith receive ye, but not to doubtful disputations.

The assignment I was given continued to plague me because I could only go so far. How many different ways could I have explained things? I thought. I couldn't give meat because they couldn't digest even the milk. I couldn't speak spiritual things because they could only comprehend carnal things. Like the saying goes, "you can take the horse to the water, but you can't make them drink," I wanted them to get it. I wanted them to understand. I wanted to ignite a passion for the Most High. Aren't they my work in the Lord? So, what does that say about me as the leader and under Sheppard?

On the inside I grew angry. I was angry with God for not giving the increase (at least a little); I was angry with myself for not being able to teach in a way that they would receive. I was also angry with that member because they didn't have a desire, passion, or ambition to seek the face of God. Years went by and we were still laying the foundation. But that was my flesh wrestling with the Spirit within me. I needed to receive them that were weak in the faith and delight myself in doing the will of the Father even if I never saw the fruits of my labor. We cannot expect those who don't know Jesus as their healer, deliverer, way-maker, or provider, to desire Him as we do or to run with the endurance as we have.

My mind would go wild trying to analyze new and innovative ways to present the gospel and "help" God do His work in them. The only problem was that God didn't need my help. He is not an analytical or logical God. Faith is what moves God and is so far from logical. Oftentimes, we may find ourselves thinking some things we are doing are for other people, when in fact, (my military friends would say) "that's YOUR exercise!"

Psychological thinking is a way for us to make sense of things. The Lord's ways are higher than our ways and are past finding out. The world and the spirit of the age gives us formulas for understanding. We say that 1+1=2, but with Jesus 1+1 can be ANYTHING! If we stop trying to put God in a box and stop limiting the ways in which we expect the Lord to operate, then we will encounter Him more and experience His miraculous works.

After you've heard all the preaching and all of the testimonies of others you'll find that you can't stand on those alone. Faith has evidence. Where is YOUR evidence? You must stand on what Jesus has done for you. I remember studying about Paul and how he started as a disciple of Christ. For a while he preached solely on the encounter he had with God on the road to Damascus. The power that he had impacted others because he believed the words he preached. The power he had was transferred to others because of the evidence. There should still be evidence of Jesus whom you can't see. This is what you hold on to from trial to trial, faith to faith as you continue to seek the face of God and grow in Him.

TEMPERANCE

2 Peter 1:5

And beside this, giving all diligence, add to your faith virtue, and to virtue knowledge;

And to knowledge temperance; and to temperance patience, and to patience godliness;

And to godliness brotherly kindness; and to brotherly kindness charity.

For if these things be in you and abound, they make you that ye shall neither be barren nor unfruitful in the knowledge of our Lord Jesus Christ.

Temperance simply put is self-control. If you do not practice self-control then we wind up grieving the Holy Spirit. As you grow to know Christ and develop a close relationship then the Holy Ghost teaches you what things to do and what not to do. There is a way that seems right to a man and the end is destruction.

Don't be quick to feed the desires of the flesh so much that you wind up putting yourself in position of needing to repent later for those actions. Think things through and ask yourself how Jesus would handle your situations or circumstances if He was in the midst of similar questionable issues. God has given angels charge over us to minister in times such as these. Utilize these angels and allow them to minister to your Spirit in trying situations. In the end, we don't want our good to be evil spoken of. Represent Jesus well; we don't want to give Him a bad reputation because of our careless or thoughtless actions.

One thing that has to be controlled the most is our mouths. Remember that we are made in the image and likeness of God. With the Spirit of God we can easily bless and curse. Don't be the author of friendly fire, or allow your mouth be an open sepulcher. Regardless of what you want to say, the Spirit should lead us to control our emotions and speak the things pleasing and edifying in the sight of God. Be angry and sin not.

Do you remember when the servants of the high priest came to arrest Jesus? A disciple was so hot-tempered that he cut the ear off of the servant and Jesus had to go behind him and fix it. Let us walk worthy of the call and be responsible with the power that God has given us. Don't put the Lord in a position of having to clean up behind a mess you've made due to lack of temperance.

Think hard and act rationally. A soldier (especially the most elite) thinks and plans with calculation and care. They consider how their every action has a possible reaction and how the strategic moves they make may affect others in their team, squadron, brigade, and so on.

I've mentioned how in previous chapters that I had somewhat of a laid back personality, shy, and seemingly standoffish. I'd see and observe lots of things some of which would upset me. I didn't do much talking but I allowed things to get bottled up from time to time and after a while something would "tip off the ice burg". Then I'd use my mouth to let them have it! I'd bring up all sorts of things that people may have done years prior. That's not how the Lord desires for us to handle things.

I admit that one of the things that bothers me is when my enemies seem to be getting a lead way or an upper hand.

Ps 37:1

> *Fret not thyself because of evildoers, neither be thou envious of workers of iniquity.*
>
> *For they shall soon be cut down like the grass, and wither as the green herb.*
>
> *Trust in the Lord and do good; so shalt thou dwell in the land, and verily thou shalt be fed.*

The Lord knows our hearts and how we process things. When the enemy comes in like a flood the Spirit of God lifts up a standard. Though our enemies may seem to prosper in their way and it puts you in a position of almost wanting to give up, we must put complete faith and trust in Jesus knowing that we're in His hands. He is our refuge. Because of this we maintain temperance and self-control. We speak the Word over and over again out of our mouths until it comes to fruition. The Word is Truth and shall not return void. Keep your mind stayed on Jesus who is the author and finisher of your faith.

When we begin to operate consistently in the Spirit, we are faced with all sorts of challenges from our enemies. Not just gossip, or desiring to see us fail, but even a desire for our demise. Nevertheless, we overcome by the blood of Jesus. The love of many may wax cold. The brotherly love and kindness will struggle to abound but perfect love never fails and in the perfected love of Christ by His Spirit we are able to maintain temperance with a pure heart until our enemies are made our foot stool.

WAITING ON THE LORD

PSALM 27:13-14

> *I had fainted unless I had believed to see the goodness of the Lord in the land of the living.*

> *Wait on the Lord: be of good courage, and He shall strengthen thine heart: wait, I say, on the Lord.*

Waiting on the Lord is sometimes one of the hardest things we must learn to do. Waiting on the Lord goes hand in hand with trust. Waiting on the Lord says that we trust that He will come to our rescue. He is our healer, our redeemer, and our refuge.

We must trust that no matter the situation or circumstance Jesus will answer us. There is no doubt that sometimes things can become confusing. However, even in times of confusion we talk to the Lord. We continue to pray and seek the Lord and in His own perfect timing He will show up. Jesus loves His children and He cares about the smallest details concerning them. He will never leave them nor forsake them.

Don't sweat the small stuff. Jesus is a healer and a way maker. He will work out all of the kinks if you allow Him to. Keep it simple and surrender to the complete will and purpose of Christ. Let Him lead and guide you by His Holy Spirit. With Him we can't go wrong. He is the God of second and third chances. Keep trusting and waiting on Him even when it doesn't seem popular.

We all can think of different situations where we needed to wait on the Lord. I've had to wait on the Lord for healing. I've had to wait on the Lord on occasion for deliverance but He always shows up with His arms stretched out. His arm is not too short that He cannot save.

Since I was a child I would often run ahead of the Spirit of God. He would give me visions and ideas and I just couldn't wait to put them into fruition. He would reveal things to me well in advance and I would have trouble understanding timing. Oftentimes, I would be led by my mind trying to figure things out and trying to "help" the Lord instead of waiting for Him to make provision for the vision.

Wait for the Lord in all things. We can't think for the Lord. We must allow Him to bring forth the increase.

I CORINTHIANS 4:18

> *While we look not at the things which are seen, but at the things which are not seen: for the things which are seen are temporal; but the things which are not seen are eternal.*

We cannot go with what our natural eye sees. When we see how things are going then it is no longer faith. Wait on the Lord. Let Him strengthen your hands. Let the weak say they are strong. His strength is made perfect in our weakness and we as the bride (His Church) must be the weaker vessel.

Sometimes we walk in unfamiliar territory where there is trouble on every side. There is stress and perils. Trials and tribulations. But we can always call on the name of Jesus who is ready and willing to save with a stretched out hand.

EPHESIANS 2:13

> *But now in Christ Jesus ye who sometimes were far off are made nigh by the blood of Christ.*
>
> *For He is our peace, who hath made both one, and hath broken down the middle partition between us.*
>
> *Having abolished in His flesh the enmity, even the law of commandments contained in ordinances; for to make in Himself of twain one new man, so making peace.*

As we do the will and purpose of Christ and stand in the ministry wherein you were called, you will find that it seems that Christ is far away sometimes. It will seem as if He is not as near but we are made near by the blood of Christ and we apply the blood of Christ in all situations gaining the victory thereby. If we draw near to Him, He will draw near to us.

Jesus is our peace and our advocate with the Father. He has taken away the walls and removed the partitions.

EPHESIANS 3:13

> *Wherefore I desire that ye faint not at my tribulations for you which is your glory.*
>
> *For this cause I bow my knees unto the Father of our Lord Jesus Christ.*
>
> *Of whom the whole family in Heaven and earth is named.*
>
> *That He would grant you, according to the riches of His glory, to be strengthened with might by His Spirit in the inner man;*

When you are believers in Christ you eat the whole loaf and be complete in Him. We cannot live in fear. We have a reverent fear as His children but we live knowing that He is the resurrection and whether we live or die in the flesh, we are His. We cannot just be hearers but we must be doers also. We must believe this completely and be found doing the will and purpose of Christ knowing that as prisoners of Christ we have a right to the tree of life. We are grafted into the vine, this vine being Christ Jesus.

I was in a situation where I was faced with several trials and tests. It seemed as if they came back to back in a short amount of time. It also seemed as if nothing was working out right. I had to seek out my own salvation with fear and much trembling. I was presented with sickness and the enemy presented me with an unhealthy, ungodly, fear of death. This sickness was not unto death but to show forth the manifest glory and power of Christ. I was doubtful at first and questioned if it was because I did something wrong. I thought I was paying the price for sins and iniquities that I committed. Therefore, I even questioned who I was in Christ. However, thanks be to the Most High God that He regulates the mind of His children.

God is not the author of confusion. Jesus desires that we prosper and be in good health. We shouldn't focus on our wrong but our focus should always be on the prize which is Christ Jesus. He is our exceedingly great reward. When we begin to see fault and wrong, we know that Christ is not the author. He chastens the ones He loves. Whether we fall short or stumble, we always want to grow from faith to faith and glory to glory trusting that Christ is leading us in every way. To God be the glory. Remember, we don't live unto ourselves. Our lives are hid in Christ (Col 3:3). We should speak life always knowing that our lives are in his hands and we belong to Christ to do as He wills.

COLOSSIANS 3:1-4

> *If ye then be risen with Christ, seek those things which are above, where Christ sitteth on the right hand of God.*
>
> *Set your affection on things above, not on things on the earth.*
>
> *For ye are dead, and your life is hid with Christ in God.*
>
> *When Christ, who is our life, shall appear, then shall ye also with Him in glory.*

We must keep our mind on the things above knowing that Jesus is our redeemer. He is our help in the time of trouble and nothing on this earth can separate us from the love of Christ. Before the foundations of the world He knew us and predestined us with purpose and mission.

MEEKNESS

What does being meek really mean? Humility. The opposite of vanity.

1 Peter 5:5-6

> *Likewise, ye younger, submit yourselves unto the elder. Yea, all of you be subject one to another, and be clothed with humility; for God resisteth the proud, and giveth grace to the humble.*
>
> *Humble yourselves therefore under the mighty hand of God that He may exalt you in due season.*

In order for the Spirit to dwell within us, death of self and the flesh is required. We are stating that "Thy will be done, O' Lord." If this truly is what we mean then we must humble ourselves and relinquish authority unto God (spoken in detail later). We relinquish our own will and ways and submit ourselves to the Most High God. It is only then that we can be most effective on the battlefield for Christ.

Humility isn't something that happens overnight. This builds with patience and as we continue to seek the face of God. All of the fruits of the Spirit will work together and function as character builders so long as you continue to let God "take the wheel."

Heb 13:7

> *Remember them which have rule over you, who have spoken unto you the Word of God: whose faith follows, considering the end of their conversation.*

One of the most difficult things for us to do is humble ourselves under those who have authority over us. As mentioned earlier, God doesn't want to humiliate us. But He does want us to trust that He can place the right people in our life to encourage us in God and to help prepare us for new levels in Christ.

It is easy to allow pride to set in and think that God will only speak to us directly. Wrong! As Christians, especially those Holy Ghost filled we must stop being so easily offended. Learn how to take rebuke and chastisement as sons of God having confidence that we are not bastards.

As the scripture says, those who have rule over us speak and impart the Word of God. Their faith follows (with evidence), and we should always consider the end of their conversation. These rulers watch for our souls and must give account before God. So like a sponge, let us absorb all that God has for us and those rulers which despitefully use us; those we must pray for.

Don't waste time thinking you can eliminate those who have rule over you. You interfere with the work God is doing in you and increase the possibility of you not being prepared for the work God has set up for you. The warfare is great, soldiers, and you must be thoroughly prepared to fight! No man is an island but where there is unity, there is strength. Let us go forth and with hope that in the end God will say "well done, thy good and faithful servant."

I remember being placed under a few leaders. Some were good experiences, and others, not so much. However, God placed me in the midst of certain leadership so that I could see what was going on in the Christian sector and to know what to do versus what not to do. There is no better training than on the job training (OJT). There are certain things you don't want to deal with but the experiences are necessary for growth.

The Lord even put me through warfare training so to speak. Fighting real demons, witches, and spiritual wickedness in high places. Those situations you can't just read about. You must experience it for yourself and put your faith to the test. No man goes to war without training. So humble yourself and know that God is your helper and your keeper.

Remember that satan was used as an example by God because he was one that thought he could eliminate and overtake the head. The end result was hell….an eternal decision. Know your position in God's army and be found in your rightful place. This is necessary to be most effective in battle and to experience true victory over the enemy.

I Cor 4:15-16

> For though ye have a thousand instructors in Christ, yet have ye not many fathers: for in Christ Jesus I have begotten you through the gospel.
>
> Wherefore I beseech you, be ye followers of me.

Keep the main thing the main thing. An instructor is an instructor. But understand that all things work together for the good. Keep your focus on the mission at all times knowing that we shall reap if we faint not.

Many have left off from being humble. If you are privileged to hear the testimony of many great leaders and pastors who've now gone astray, they would say that they, too, had humble beginnings. Nevertheless, the spirit of vanity pursued them and conquered (though they won't admit it).

Though the Spirit of God is in operation, it is often difficult to stay focused. Somehow many may focus on the vessel being used instead of focusing on the Spirit of the Most High God speaking through that vessel. God has all the power! On our own, we are nothing. No flesh can move God.

There are times and seasons for everything, and now is the time to dress for the job. One of the greatest controversies surrounding the ministry Jesus had when he walked the earth was that He did not look like a king. However, He did dress for the job and that work He was doing which could be summed up as warfare. Just as a police officer has a uniform and a fire fighter has a certain attire; so do we. We too, must dress for the job and put on the whole armor. Many of the people that will receive you are those who have a hunger and thirst after righteousness. They have a desire for the Spirit of Truth so much that they won't care which form it comes or the vessel used to bring it. It's never about us. The enemy will try to deceive us and have us rationalize what the Word of God says. We are the garbage men. We take out the trash that the devil has created in the lives of many. The time is not yet to put on the royal attire when there is still so much work left to do.

I Corinthians 9:19-22

> *For though I be free from all men, yet have I made myself servant unto all, that I might gain the more.*
>
> *And unto the Jews I became as a Jew that I might gain the Jews; to them that are under the law, that I might gain them that are under the law;*
>
> *To them that are without the law, as without the law, (being not without law to God, but under the law to Christ,) that I might gain them that are without law.*
>
> *To the weak became I as weak, that I might gain the weak: I am made all things to all men that I might by all means save some.*

So we ought to humble ourselves with confidence in who we are, knowing our reward in Christ. Yet, we become what we need to be to get the job done and carry out the mission Christ has given us to fulfil. We become all things to all men to by all means save some.

We now live in a generation of stiff-necked people, many of whom are being led by the spirit of the age. We must not lose focus because of the people and what's going on around us. There is great wickedness that surrounds us but it is important to remain humble and finish the course. If you operate with the need to prove to people who you are, you will fail. If you have a need for recognition, you will fail. At no time is this walk about us. We must die! We must lose ourselves...not just sometimes but all of the time!

There will always be great opposition when it comes to doing the works of the Lord. Nevertheless, remember that Jesus has already set the standard for us. Think back for a moment when Jesus walked the earth. The majority of the opposition actually came from the church (religious sector). There wasn't a whole lot of opposition from the non-believer. The major opposers were the Pharisees, Sadducees, and the Scribes; those well skilled in the law. So expect opposition but don't allow it to throw you off course. Let the Spirit bear witness for you with the works of confirmation following.

I can remember when I first answered the call on my life to pastorship. The Lord told my husband and I to go forth with ministry. We started with a radio broadcast and soon after, leased a building. We operated in obedience and humility, speaking the truth boldly with confidence. No one called into our radio broadcast; there were no praise reports or testimonies. No one wanted to sow into our ministry. We were shunned and outcast. I was even told and treated like I was too young. Many days I preached to the walls because no one showed up for service. I humbly asked the Lord what was going on. What was the point? Why would He tell me to do something that wouldn't work? Broadcast after broadcast people would throw slurs, "you're not a pastor, where is your flock?" I went to the Lord with the same question. "Where is my flock? Why do you call me pastor without giving me a flock?" The Lord responded, "Pastor, you do have a flock. It is not a traditional ministry I have given you. Your flock will not always be seen. You have a radio flock and an internet flock. Soon you will do conferences. I am doing a new thing and I don't need another church building to do it. Did I tell you to go and lease a building?"

When I heard these words I was comforted, but for six years I went forth with radio, internet, conferences, and writing. We also went to hospitals and nursing homes, along with some speaking engagements. In warfare terms, we considered ourselves a covert operation; special ops. The majority of the judgment work and warfare was done under the radar and behind the scenes. It wasn't what I wanted to do, but it was what I was called to do. Throughout the entire time I was seeing things and learning the warfare, learning the precepts of the Most High and how to fight.

Many whom I met in ministry and called themselves friends (though I called them acquaintances), thought that I was crazy. They felt that I was unlearned and didn't have a clue. It angered me to know these things. I had been given many gifts and talents. Most of all, I had the power of the Holy Ghost. I felt like people were taking my gentleness, kindness, and humility as if it were for weakness. Several pastors and apostles approached me and told me to stop what I was doing. "Come humble yourself under my ministry for a few years. You can be my assistant," they would say. My flesh got fed up many times and I wanted to show them who God really was in me. However, the Spirit of God within me said, "elevate beyond these situations and circumstances, do my will. Those who need to see what I've done in you will see, but now is the time to elevate and do my work. Stay focused on the mission and be an "undertaker" of the devil!"

The Lord knew what He called me to do. I knew what He called me to do and it was necessary to continue in confidence and boldness. I had to trust God and walk by faith and in obedience, knowing that He who began a good work in me would perform it until the day of Jesus Christ (Phil 1:6). The Lord is the author and the finisher of our faith. Jesus knew that He was King when He came to die once for all to give us a chance for salvation. Humility kept Him on that cross even when many couldn't and would never comprehend. He became all things to all men so that by all means He may save some.

THE BLOOD OF JESUS...AND ITS PURITY

ROMANS 2:24-25

> *Being justified freely by His grace through the redemption that is in Christ Jesus:*

> *Whom God hath set forth to be a propitiation through faith in His blood, to declare His righteousness for the remission of sins that are past, through the forbearance of God;*

ROMANS 5:8-9

> *But God commendeth His love toward us, in that, while we were yet sinners, Christ died for us.*

> *Much more then, being now justified by His blood, we shall be saved from wrath through Him.*

I JOHN 5:5

> *Who is He that overcometh the World, but He that believeth that Jesus is the son of God?*

> *This is He that came by water and blood, even Jesus Christ; not by water only, but by water and blood. And it is the Spirit that beareth witness, because the Spirit is Truth.*

Though we may be talking about the power given by the Spirit of God, we must first acknowledge that there could be no such power without there first being a shedding of blood. Jesus became that ultimate sacrifice, humbling himself unto death through the shedding of His blood. It is because of His purified blood that was shed that we now have access to the power of the Holy Spirit.

We must believe that Jesus' love was perfected on the cross and that His blood was shed for the remission of our sins. Therein is the Power of Christ by His Spirit. Remember that water is symbolic of His Spirit but He came not by water only but by water and blood. It's all because of the blood!

How can you go forth in the power and authority given by His Spirit if you're not first cleansed by the blood? It is not a small thing but the blood of Jesus is the main thing. We have victory because of the blood. We have joy because of the blood. We have freedom because of the blood. We have access to the promise and all good things because of the blood...and the list goes on.

As you know, we were birthed into a spiritual battle. Spiritual warfare continues day by day. In the Spirit the battle is already won and it's because of the blood of Jesus. The power is in His blood and its how we conquer our enemy and triumph through situations and circumstances that may come our way. Our hope is in the blood.

REVELATION 12:11

And they overcame Him by the blood of the lamb, and by the Word of their testimony; and they loved not their lives unto the death.

Our overcoming power is in the blood of Jesus. Therein we must lean and depend. For our weapons or warfare are not carnal but mighty to the pulling down of strongholds. The blood is what washes and cleanses us and puts us in a place of righteousness before the Lord so we are able to stand and contend for the faith. We operate effectively in the Spirit and prevail because of the confidence established with the shedding of His blood. The Spirit and the blood are one. Though the Lord greatly desires for us to receive His Holy Spirit, He also wants us to know the depths of His love given through His blood.

The Name of Jesus

There is power in the name of Jesus. By this name every knee shall bow and every tongue shall confess that Jesus Christ is Lord. He is the Alpha and Omega. He is the first and the last. He is the beginning and the end.

He exceeds all wisdom and knowledge of this world. There is no name greater. If you're ever in a situation or circumstance beyond human comprehension you can just call on the name of Jesus. Jesus is the only name I know. There is no other name.

Jesus! There is no way to the Father except through the son. Jesus is the way, the Truth, and the Life.

Revelation 12:11

And they overcame Him by the blood of the Lamb, and by the word of their testimony; and they loved not their lives unto the death.

Jesus is not dead. He is risen! We must carry our lives like God is not dead. No matter what the enemy does to trick or fool us. We renew our minds all throughout the day and call on the name of Jesus in times of trouble. The enemy will try to have us contradict what the Word of God says but we cast down every vain imagination that exalts itself above the knowledge of God, over and over again. We cling to the words that have been spoken out of the mouth of God.

Jesus cannot be defeated. We call on His name in every circumstance knowing that He is our helper and our keeper.

John 6:35

> And Jesus said unto them, I am the bread of Life. He that cometh to me shall never hunger; and He that believeth on me shall never thirst.

We hunger and thirst after righteousness and eat of the bread of life which is Christ Jesus. He is the author and finisher of our faith and the author of all life. He said that we have a spiritual hunger and thirst which can be filled by Him. If we come to Him, we will never want. By His name is the provision made for His people. Let's make it clear that the price has already been paid. He shed His blood and died on the cross so that there was a sacrifice once for all.

John 11:25

> *Jesus said unto her, I am the resurrection, and the life: He that believeth in me, though he were dead, yet shall he live;*
>
> *And whosoever liveth and believe in me shall never die. Believest thou this?*

We must believe the words that have been spoken and written by the Lord and use His name throughout every situation and circumstance as if our lives depend on it, because it does! His name is why we move and have our being.

Grace and Mercy

Romans 5:19-23

For if by one man's offence death reigned by one; much more they which receive abundance of grace and of the gift of righteousness shall reign in life by one, Jesus Christ.

Therefore as by the offence of one judgment came upon all men to condemnation; even so by the righteousness of one the free gift came upon all men unto justification of life.

For as by one man's disobedience many were made sinners, so by the obedience of one shall many be made righteous.

Moreover the law entered, that the offence might abound. But where sin abounded, grace did much more abound:

That as sin hath reigned unto death, even so might grace reign through righteousness unto eternal life by Jesus Christ our Lord.

Thank Jesus for His grace and for His mercy! When you truly love the Lord, you have a desire to please Him, as the first commandment says with all thy heart, mind, and soul. It is natural to not want to fall short but we all fall short of the glory of God because of sin. There is none righteous. But that is exactly what the Lord has given us grace for.

We grow form faith to faith, glory to glory, abounding in grace, hope and love. Jesus is our hope and our righteousness. We must remember we are no longer under the law but we are under grace because of our relationship and reconciliation with Christ. There is nothing we can do on our own (though this may contrary to popular belief). We need the Holy Spirit to lead and guide us into the path of holiness and righteousness. When you attempt to do things on your own, in your own strength then you are establishing your own righteousness which we know is self-righteousness.

Rom 10:3-4

> For they being ignorant of God's righteousness, and going about to establish their own righteousness, had not submitted themselves unto the righteousness of God.
>
> For Christ is the end of the law for righteousness to everyone that believeth.

Our righteousness must be established in Christ. Thank God for His obedience even to the death on the cross! Through our offences death reigns, but through obedience and righteousness and through belief in Christ comes the abundance of grace and the justification of life.

When I really met Christ He captured my heart completely. There was a passionate pursuit that birthed in me. The more I sought Him, the more in love I was. There was a hunger and a thirsting (and still is) that couldn't be quenched by anything but His Spirit. I wanted more of Him in every way. However, with all of this there was a desire to walk uprightly before Him. There was a self-consciousness that was unhealthy. I wanted to dot every I and cross every T. Every time I did slip or fall, I stumbled and stumbled not willing to accept the grace that came with being a believer. However, this is what His grace is for! We don't practice sin or intentionally do things contrary to the Word of God but because we have sin nature we do these things. Because of His grace we can cry to the Lord with godly sorrow and repentance and He is faithful to forgive us of our transgressions and iniquities.

Ps 32:1&5

> *Blessed is He whose transgression is forgiven, whose sin is covered.*

> *I acknowledged my sin unto thee, and mine iniquity have I not hid. I said, I will confess my transgressions unto the Lord; and thou forgavest the iniquity of my sin.*

Thank you Jesus for your grace, mercy, and compassion. He is a God that is able to do all things but fail. There is no failure in Christ. However, we must surrender our own will and allow Him to lead us by His Holy Spirit. He will not lead you in the wrong direction. Sometimes things may get a little uncomfortable but that's when we trust Him walking by faith knowing that He is our helper, keeper, and way maker.

I Peter 2:9-10

But ye are a chosen generation, royal priesthood, a Holy nation, a peculiar people; that ye should shew forth the praises of Him who hath called you out of darkness into His marvelous light.

Which in time past were not a people, but are now the people of God: which had not obtained mercy, but now have obtained mercy.

We are a new generation of believers chosen to show forth Christ along with His miracles, signs, and wonders. Though we weren't chosen before in the old letter, now through the grace and mercy of Christ we have obtained this redemption. What favor!

Romans 9:15

> *For He saith to Moses, I will have mercy on whom I will have mercy, and I will have compassion on whom I will have compassion.*

So then it is not of him that willeth, nor of Him that runneth, but of God that sheweth mercy.

Grace, mercy, and compassion are distributed by the Lord as He wills. Thank Jesus for His mercy. We receive mercy whether we are inside or outside of the will of Christ. Meaning that whether we saved or not, in His mercy we find favor and life. Jesus covers us, shields and protects us even during those times when we are not seeking after righteousness or holiness. There are many times we find that we have become distracted and have lost focus on the main thing which is Christ. Still the Lord blankets us with His mercy, compassion, patience, and long suffering.

Rom 9:21

Hath not the potter power over the clay, of the same lump to make one vessel unto honor, and another unto dishonor?

What if God, willing to shew His wrath, and to make His power known, endureth with much long suffering the vessels of wrath fitted to destruction:

And that He might make known the riches of His glory on the vessels of mercy, which He had afore prepared unto glory?

For a long period of time I would beat myself up for mistakes that I had made because I was so hard on myself and greatly wanted to please the Lord. I wasn't walking in the grace that came along with the gift of salvation. It was foolish and self-righteous of me.

The Lord wants us to learn and grow by our faults. This is why He desires for us to come to Him as children. No matter the situation or the circumstance children are complexly dependent on their parent and have no doubt that things will work out like they should. Likewise, we should have that same assurance which is given by His precious Spirit. However, saying all of this, we must let his Spirit reign and quench it not.

True worship is birthed in appreciation for such a grace given by His Spirit. We don't take advantage of His grace but it is there as a cushion for us if we so happen to slip on occasion.

So walk with confidence knowing what it means to be graced by Him. Acknowledge Him in all of your ways and He will direct your path. Allow the Spirit to guide you and you'll know that your footsteps are ordered of the Lord.

Remember there is nothing we can do to be worthy of His grace and mercy but because of the depths of His love towards us He looks past our faults and meets our every need.

Mercy says that regardless of the situation or the circumstance I'm going to allow you to live. Mercy says I will still honor you as sons and daughters. Mercy says I'm still going to bless you, I'm going to keep you. Wow! What a privilege to have mercy given by His Spirit.

> *Therefore seeing that we have this ministry as we have received mercy we faint not; but have renounced the hidden things of dishonesty, not walking in craftiness, nor handling the Word of God deceitfully; but by manifestation of the truth commending ourselves to every man's conscience in the sight of God.*
>
> *For we preach not ourselves but Christ Jesus the Lord; and ourselves your servants for Jesus' sake.*
>
> *But we have this treasure in earthen vessels, that the excellency of the power may be of God, and not of us.*
>
> *For our light affliction which is but for a moment, worketh for us a far more exceeding and eternal weight of Glory.*

How great is the mercy that the Lord God has shown unto us. We have received His mercy and because of this we are strengthened to persevere. We are overcomers by the blood of the lamb and each new day we are given which is filled with grace and compassion, we move to keep fighting and to keep seeking after the Spirit of God.

The Lord shows mercy on whom He wills and compassion on whom He wills and the blessing is that He is our exceedingly great reward. We go forth trying to show forth the works of Christ which are no longer dead works but works of faith, not laying again the same foundation.

II CORINTHIAN 7:8-10

> *For though I made you sorry with a letter, I do not repent though I did repent for I perceive that the same epistle hath made you sorry though it were but for a season.*

> *Now I rejoice not that ye were made sorry but that ye sorrowed to repentance: for ye were made sorry after a godly manner that ye might receive damage by us for nothing.*

> *For Godly sorrow worketh repentance to salvation not to be repented of but the sorrow of the world worketh death.*

> *For He hath made Him to be sin for us, who knew no sin; that we might be made righteousness of God in Him.*

When I was a young adult I would do a lot of traveling back and forth to visit family that lived about 4.5 hours away. One weekend after visiting I got on the road really late. I admit that I acknowledged the Lord as my Savior but I was heavy laden in sin. I began driving thinking that I could make it to my destination but after about two hours there seemed to be a spirit of slumber that came upon me. I started to weave then the Holy Spirit took the wheel. I woke up the next morning well rested in my bed. I don't remember how I made it home or even getting into bed. I didn't pray before I left and I didn't pray when I woke up. But His mercy endured. There are so many faults...but His mercy endures!

FORGIVENESS

MARK11:25

And when ye stand praying forgive, if ye have aught against any: that your father also which is in Heaven may forgive you your trespasses.

But if ye do not forgive, neither will your father which is in Heaven forgive your trespasses.

Forgiveness may seem to be a light thing but it is extremely significant regarding Jesus Christ and His plan of Salvation. We cannot receive redemption if our sins and transgressions without first forgiving those that may have trespassed against us. Once you forgive others, be sure to forgive yourself as well.

I happened to be in ministry for well over seven years when the Lord decided to humble me...again. I knew all about humility and humbling myself at the mighty hand of God but I still had secret faults. Deep in my heart I had not yet given everything completely over to Jesus. I needed to lay aside EVERY weight, care, and burden. I was burdened with guilt of my past and was still holding on to childhood hurts and pains. All of this was hidden and suppressed. I loved my parents and my family but I subconsciously still wanted to see them struggle a little for what happened to me. When I say struggle, I mean emotionally I wanted to actually see the remorse. This was wrong! When you truly forgive, the purified love of Christ shines and you don't desire to linger on that situation. Thank Jesus for the revelation and that when it's made known we can make adjustments accordingly.

Psalm 51:10

> *Create in me a clean heart, O God; and renew a right spirit within me.*

We must cleanse ourselves completely of old things and those things which we could not control. True forgiveness means that we have cast it into the sea of forgetfulness. We don't desire for punishment or demise but we have desire for grace, mercy, salvation, and endure with longsuffering, praying for those who despitefully use us and keep our eyes on the prize.

Psalm 32:1&5

> *Blessed is He whose transgression is forgiven, whose sin is covered.*

> *I acknowledged my sin unto thee, and mine iniquity have I not hid. I said, I will confess my transgressions unto the Lord; and thou forgavest the iniquity of my sin.*

If we want our sins to be covered we must also have a desire for the sins of others to be covered. We repent and turn from our sin and we should do the same for our brothers and sisters. At no time should we have a desire to make their sins publicly known. Jesus died that we may cover sins and have the right to the tree of life.

In the account of Noah in His drunkenness, He became uncovered and His son saw His nakedness. The one son desired to make it known to the other brothers. However, the brothers went in backward and covered Him. This is why it is so important to walk in the Spirit. The Spirit is our covering and He doesn't desire for our demise or humiliation but for reconciliation and forgiveness.

Don't hold onto things. Jesus is our advocate with the Father. He is our burden bearer. Give Him your cares for His yoke is easy and His burden is light. Confess your sins unto the Lord so that He may cleanse you and make you whole. The debt for sin has already been paid on the cross.

TRUST

PSALMS 25:1-2

> *Unto thee, O Lord do I lift up my soul. O my God, I trust in thee: Let me not be ashamed, let not mine enemies triumph over me.*

Psalms 7:1

> *O Lord my God, in thee do I put my trust: save me from all them that persecute me, and deliver me.*

Trust and faith are the very keys to your redemption. We cannot proclaim to know the true and living God without faith and trust. In other chapters on faith we discussed miracles as faith builders. Trust is particularly the same. We must trust that Jesus has our best interest at heart. We must trust that He knows what He is doing. His ways are higher than our ways and His thoughts are higher than our thoughts. All power originates from Him. All things have been created for Him and by Him and there is none who can take us out of His hands.

Sometimes we stumble but we grow from faith to faith and from glory to glory. Faith comes by hearing and hearing by the Word of God (Rom 10:17). It is good to hear the testimonies of the saints of God so that we grow in faith thereby. We also build trust by overcoming trials and tribulations. The Lord never puts more on us than we can bear. All things work together for the good of them that Love the Lord.

There was a time in my life when I thought I was standing tall in Christ. The Lord would often remind me to stand tall because I didn't always walk in the boldness and the confidence He instructed me to walk in. I knew His Word and had a zeal and passion to share it with anyone who would listen. However, I lacked confidence because of numerous occasions of rejection. I didn't look the part. I seemed to be too young or not educated enough. But the question remained, would I be obedient to do what the Lord instructed and trust that He was with me through the things I encountered?

II Corinthians 6:4-10

> But in all things approving ourselves as the ministers of God in much patience, in afflictions, in necessities, in distresses,
>
> In stripes, in imprisonments, in tumults, in labours, in watchings, in fastings;
>
> By pureness, by knowledge, by longsuffering, by kindness, by the Holy Ghost, by love unfeigned,
>
> By the Word of Truth, by the Power of God, by the armour of righteousness, on the right hand and on the left,
>
> By honour and dishonor, by evil report and good report: as deceivers, and yet true;
>
> As unknown, and yet well known; as dying, and behold, we live; as chastened, and not killed;
>
> As sorrowful, yet always rejoicing; as poor, yet making many rich; as having nothing, and yet possessing all things.

I must admit my trouble regarding this scripture. We must trust that through all things including perils and all sorts of long sufferings that we are still in the righteousness of Christ. There were numerous tests and trials I encountered where I questioned if I was suffering for righteousness sake or for foolishness. I couldn't always stand in the trust with boldness and confidence because I wasn't sure if I was righteous.

Please understand that we as believers who are covered by the Holy Spirit and apply the blood of Jesus to our life will always be walking in holiness and righteousness. That's what faith and trust is all about. We acknowledge the Lord in all of our ways and He will direct our path. Don't allow mind binding spirits to convince you otherwise. As believers our faith is counted as righteousness and we must stand in that fact.

We also will fall short of the glory of God where those things listed in the above scripture will apply to our lives. However, we make adjustments, we hold ourselves accountable one toward another taking responsibility for our actions confessing our faults and forgiving one another.

REDEMPTION

ROMANS 3:23-24

> *For all have sinned, and come short of the glory of God:*
>
> *Being justified freely by His grace through the redemption that is in Christ Jesus:*
>
> *Whom God had set forth to be a propitiation through faith in His blood, to declare His righteousness for the remission of sins that are past, through the forbearance of God;*

We cannot do anything without Jesus. Jesus is our redeemer. We all fall short of His glory but through faith in His blood our transgressions are covered and righteousness is restored.

Don't give up hope because your emotions get the best of you and tell you that you've done too much wrong to be forgiven. Don't be tricked. Don't be fooled. We are freely justified by His grace. This means that this grace is not distributed in limited portions but by faith and in the blood of Christ He is faithful to pour His grace upon liberally upon His children who desire to accomplish His will.

He's already paid the price. Jesus has endured every temptation and affliction imaginable. You must walk in faith knowing you're redeemed by His blood and that the tests and trials come make us stronger in the faith.

I THESSALONIANS 3:3

> *That no man should be moved by these afflictions: for yourselves know that we are appointed thereunto.*

We should consider it a privilege when the trying of our faith comes knowing that the Lord considers us worthy to endure for His names' sake. We don't take this lightly but we should pour our worship upon His feet simply because we cannot fathom the depth or height of love He has for us to have even paid such a price.

ROMANS 5:6-8

> For when we were yet without strength, in due time Christ died for the ungodly.
>
> For scarcely for a righteous man will one die: yet peradventure for a good man some would even dare to die.
>
> But God commendeth His love toward us, in that, while we were yet sinners, Christ died for us.

You must be drawn and because you're reading this we know that you were. Now you must maintain the boldness and confidence given by His Spirit to continue to draw closer and closer.

The Spirit of God is a promise that comes along with the precious gift of redemption. Our works and actions should be a demonstration of such a gift compelling others to desire a relationship with Christ as well. I believe this is the reason Paul was led to write I Corinthians 2:4.

> And my speech and my preaching was not enticing words of man's wisdom. But in demonstration of the Spirit and of power:
>
> We must freely as Christ has also freely given to us.
>
> It is difficult to demonstrate or put forth actions of things we haven't seen or done before. This is one of the reason Jesus came and set the standard for us. How can someone demonstrate acts of love, kindness, and gentleness if they haven't seen it before? Yet it is given by His Spirit, We, as "the village" must continue to maintain these standards set forth by Christ.

PATIENCE AND HOPE

ROMANS 5:3

And not only so, but we glory in tribulations also; knowing that tribulation worketh patience; and patience, experience, and experience, hope:

And hope maketh not ashamed; because the love of God is shed abroad in our hearts by the Holy Ghost which is given unto us.

For when we were yet without strength, in due time Christ died for the ungodly.

Jesus came as the high priest to save us from sins. We can call on the name of Jesus and He will come to the rescue. He is our rock and our fortress, a present help in the time of trouble.

By His Spirit we are able to wait patiently on the Lord.

For men verily swear by the greater: and an oath for confirmation is to them an end of all strife.

Wherein God, willing more abundantly to shew unto the heirs of promise the immutability of His counsel, confirmed it by an oath: that by two immutable things, in which it was impossible for God to lie, we might have a strong consolation who have fled for refuge to lay hold upon the hope set before us. Which hope we have as an anchor of the soul, both sure and steadfast and which entereth into that within the veil:

Whither the forerunner is for us entered, even Jesus, made an high priest forever after the order of Melchisedec.

The word of Christ is true and shall not return void. Believe the word and its completion. Man shall not live by bread alone: but by every word that proceeds out of the mouth of God. By this word we have hope and this hope is life.

GALATIANS 5:1

Stand fast therefore in the liberty wherewith Christ hath made us free, and be not entangled again with the yoke of bondage.

For we through the Spirit wait for the hope of righteousness and faith.

Jesus is our hope and our righteousness. His name is faith. Our patience and hope by obedience shall bring forth a fruitful harvest. For as we know this harvest is plentiful but the laborers are few.

We must allow the Holy Spirit to breakdown the flesh and have these fruits reign in completion. The Spirit is what allows for the building and growth of these fruits but we must allow the Spirit of God to do the work.

FASTING

MARK 2:19-20

And Jesus said unto them, Can the children of the bride chamber fast, while the bridegroom is with them? As long as they have the bridegroom with them, they cannot fast.

But the days will come when the bridegroom shall be taken away from them, and then shall they fast in those days.

The great thing about having the Spirit of God is that His presence is with you at all times. Nothing can separate us. However, sin can put us in a position to where we really don't feel His manifest presence as we would like to. Sometimes we may pray for the Lord to remove some things and break some habits but sometimes the Lord requires more such as turning over the plate.

Nothing is natural. Everything is spiritual. We are spiritual beings. Just like we have a natural flesh, we have a spiritual flesh. Sometimes the shedding of flesh is necessary to get to that place that the Lord desires you to be. This is when a fast is necessary.

When a person receives the Holy Spirit there are still some things that the Lord is dealing with them about. Though the Lord is there as the comforter, the feelings such as loneliness may still be present. There is great desire to feel His presence near. Then you may inquire of the Lord about a possible fast asking about how many days and letting Him know the reason. Be sure you know the reason. We don't fast just to feel His presence. Praise is what we do to have His manifest presence. The fasting is to break down flesh and to break away from the bondage of sin. The feeling of His presence then becomes natural as holiness and righteousness continues to abound.

PRAISE AND WORSHIP

JOHN 4:23-24

> But the hour cometh and now is when the true worshippers shall worship the Father in Spirit and in Truth: For the Father seeketh such to worship Him.
>
> God is a Spirit and they that worship Him must worship in Spirit and in Truth.

Praise and worship is a powerful tool and weapon of warfare. It's not just to lift up the name of Jesus but therein you will also find strength. Praise is the answer to every problem, situation, and circumstance. The Lord inhabits the praises of His people.

Isaiah 61:1-3

> The Spirit of the Lord God is upon me; because He hath anointed me to preach good tidings unto the meek; He hath sent me to bind up the broken hearted, to proclaim liberty to the captives, and the opening of the prison to them that are bound;
>
> To proclaim the acceptable year of our Lord, and the day of vengeance of our God; to comfort all that mourn; to appoint unto them that mourn in Zion, to give unto them beauty for ashes, the oil of joy for mourning, the garment of praise for the spirit of heaviness; that they might be called trees of righteousness, the planting of the Lord, that He might be glorified.

Praise heals. Praise delivers. Praise sets captives free. Praise lifts the spirit of heaviness. No matter the situation, no matter the circumstance. Jesus is always there and you're able to feel His manifest presence through your praise and worship. Praise cleanses and draws you closer to Christ.

JOHN 12:32

And I, If I be lifted up from the earth, will draw all men unto me.

The more we lift up the name of Jesus, the more the Lord draws us closer and has us to rise above troubles, and trials from our everyday lives. He is our refuge going through circumstances with us, every burden, every care, brokenness and the praise gives us confirmation of this fact.

The Spirit searches all things, even the very deep things of God. The heart cannot lie to the Spirit. It must be pure, true worship of the Most High. Full surrender is required. We must decrease and He must increase. We must get lost in our praise and become one with Him in the Spirit. In the Spirit is where we must be. It is there that the captives are set free and yokes broken.

Your praise confuses the enemy. You are strengthened to stand and to continue to contend for the faith. Your praises scatter the enemy's devices. It is through praise that you can communicate with the Lord and receive intel about your enemies.

Praise Him without the music. It's okay to praise without music. The Spirit of God has His own rhythm. Become one with the Spirit in your praise and you'll move with the rhythm given by the Holy Spirit anyway. Don't wait until you get to church. You are the church. Praise Him now!

PRAYING IN THE SPIRIT

EPHESIANS 6:18

> *Praying always with all prayer and supplications in the spirit, and watching thereunto with all perseverance and supplication for all saints,*

II TIMOTHY 1:7

> *For God hath not given us the spirit of fear; but of power, and of love, and of a sound mind.*

To be most effective in our daily walk with Christ we must have a consistent prayer life, praying without ceasing. When we receive the Holy Spirit the Lord also gifts us with our prayer language giving us the ability to speak in another tongue. This prayer language also gives us means to fellowship and communicate with the Lord as well as other saints in the Spirit without interference from the enemy.

Romans 8:26

> *Likewise the Spirit also helpeth our infirmities: for we know not what we should pray as we ought: but the Spirit itself maketh intercession for us with groanings which cannot be uttered.*

> *And He that searcheth the hearts knoweth what is the mind of the Spirit, because He maketh intercession for the saints according to the will of God.*

Sometimes when we go into our prayer closet we may already know much of what we are going to pray about. However, if we pray in the Spirit we are sure we are praying the Lord's will because the Spirit intercedes on our behalf praying those things to the Father that we don't know to pray or we don't think of. This is one of the ways the Spirit helps bear our infirmities.

In Daniel we've read about how he had prayed and that his prayers, though they were heard, they were help up by the enemy. However, we recognize that we've been granted an awesome privilege having access to the Holy Spirit. This tool and weapon of warfare allows us to pray prayers to the Most High with expectation of a rapid response because the enemy has no understanding of this method of communication.

James 5:16

> *Confess your faults one to another, and pray one for another, that ye may be healed. The effectual fervent prayers of a righteous man availeth much.*

We've heard this scripture on numerous occasions and we understand that the Lord knows what we stand in need of even before we ask. Do we really grasp the concept that the effectual fervent prayer is what avails? This means that we are praying our heart. We don't just pray once and leave it there but we continue in prayer for the saints of God.

Though we may often be on the receiving end, it is just as important that you, too, become a "prayer warrior". There are other saints within the body of Christ that need our prayers just as much as we need theirs. Let love abound with true heartfelt prayers one for another. We all have different administrations of gifts but when it comes to prayer that is a responsibility of all of the saints of God. Please don't tell someone you're praying for them if you're not. This is a "labor" of love and a great necessity throughout the body. We don't give up. We're effectual ad fervent until healing comes or deliverance comes. Remember if one of us suffers as a member, we all suffer bearing the infirmities of one another.

I Corinthians 12:26

> *And whether one member suffers, all the members suffer*
> *with it; or one member be honoured, all the member*
> *rejoice with it.*

There are people we hear about who may sick or shut-in. We
hear of brothers and sisters in the faith who may have lost their
jobs or are having struggles. When the Lord allows us to hear of
such things love should have us immediately get on our knees
and pray them through. Consistently. Effectually. Fervently. Daily.
Hourly. Not only are we helpers of one another but we are one
so we pray for them as if we would pray for ourselves.

Matthew 21:22

> *And all things, whatsoever ye shall ask in prayer,*
> *believing, ye shall receive.*

Don't just go through the motions. Cleanse yourself in prayer
before praying for others. Don't just pray to "get it over with".
We pray in sincerity of heart and truly hoping that situations will
change for the better. If you're praying your brother gets a better
job, "do you really want that for him? Do you want him to get
promoted? Do want him to afford a new home?" We must mean
it praying in the Spirit under the power and authority given by
Christ.

I can recall a time when I was hospitalized. Though I prayed as
best as I could with the little strength that I did have, I must
admit I needed some assistance from some prayer warriors.
Where were they? Thank God for my husband loving me and
praying me through. I don't know if I've experienced a more
lonely time. My enemies were happy to hear of the situation but
those that claimed to be on the battlefield must have been too
busy.

We shouldn't be so busy with natural things that we aren't doing our job spiritually. There are lots of responsibilities that we all have, especially those blessed with large families. However, we must prioritize the spiritual. We should be teaching our children to pray and call on the name of Jesus as well. Become passionate about it. To whom much is given, much is required and as much as you may think otherwise, salvation is a big thing. The time that it takes to gossip about a situation is the same amount of time that you could be praying about It. Which one is more effective or beneficial? Which one glorifies God?

I Corinthians 14:14-15

> *For if I pray in an unknown tongue, my spirit prayeth, but my understanding is unfruitful. What is it then? I will pray with the Spirit and I will pray with the understanding also:*

In all thy getting we must get an understanding. We must pray the will of God. In prayer we come to Him with a reverence, first believing that He is. We're believing that He is the creator of all things, He sees all, He knows all, and He's able to do all things but fail.

A PURIFIED MIND

Finally, brethren, whatsoever things are true, whatsoever things are honest, whatsoever things are just, whatsoever things are pure, whatsoever things are lovely, whatsoever things are of good report; if there be any virtue, and if there be any praise, think on these things.

I Corinthians 2:15-16

> But He that is spiritual judgeth all things, yet he himself is judged of no man.
>
> For who hath known the mind of the Lord, that He may instruct him? But we have the mind of Christ.

Everyday we get up we must start out with a refreshed, renewed mind. By the Holy Spirit we are given the privilege of having the mind of Christ. This is the only way to have the mind of the Lord in the Spirit.

The scripture urges us to think on things that are true and worthy of praise. Where your mind is often filters to the heart and we want our heart and mind to be cleansed and renewed daily.

Romans 12:1-2

> I beseech you therefore brethren, by the mercies of God, that ye present your bodies a living sacrifice, holy, acceptable unto God, which is your reasonable service.
>
> And be not conformed to this world: but be ye transformed by the renewing of your mind, that ye may prove what is that good and acceptable, and perfect, will of God.

For I say, through the grace given unto me, to every man that is among you, not to think of himself more highly than he ought to think; but to think soberly, according as God hath dealt to every man he measure of faith.

It has often been said that the mind is a battlefield. We are in spiritual war and we must maintain a renewed mind in Christ to be victorious. This is the will of Christ. This is a part of presenting ourselves unto Christ as a living sacrifice.

With a mind of Christ and the things of Christ we find our strength in Christ. We must give our all to Christ. Just when you think you can't do it you find that you can do all things through Christ who strengthens you. But you must allow Him to strengthen you! He will not allow you to fail. There is no failure in Christ. No buts about it!

CHAPTER III

GIFTS OF THE SPIRIT

GIFTS OF THE SPIRIT

The Holy Spirit is a gift in itself. However, once you have the gift of the Holy Ghost it distributes certain gifts as it wills (1Cor 12:11). These gifts are to be used specifically for the building of the Kingdom of God and for the edification of the saints.

The gifts of the Spirit are the words of wisdom, word of knowledge, faith, healing, and miracles, prophesy, discerning of spirits, diverse kinds of tongues, and interpretation of tongues (1Cor 12:8-10). These gifts of the Spirit are without repentance. So this means that whether one backslides or not, the gift is still within them and available for use.

WORD OF WISDOM

The Word of Wisdom is a gift on its own but will often be seen in operation by prophets or those with the gift of prophesy. In order to understand the gift of the Word of Wisdom you must first know what wisdom means. The simplest definition of wisdom is the effective application of knowledge.

An example of this would be: your car's gas light flashes on stating that the tank is running empty. Wisdom would tell you the time to get gas is now rather than later. Someone utilizing their gift of wisdom may simply give you instructions on how to apply what you already know. For example, you know you want to own your own business. Wisdom tells you how to go about doing it.

Early in my life I was blessed with the gift of wisdom and at times I found it difficult to put into words things in a way others could understand. For the longest period of time I didn't recognize it as a gift because with this gift comes the ability to do anything (for me anyway).

I've always loved math and science, and had a passion for helping others. So the jobs I've held early in life ranged from accounting, bookkeeping, telemarketing, collections, mortgage broker, on to emergency med tech, nursing, and nearly everything in between! My analytical mind pondered on these things and often I had become so frustrated with what seemed to be indecisiveness.

Finally, I went before the Lord after five years in ministry and after establishing three businesses, and cried. "Lord, what is it that you really want me to do? I wish I could narrow it down to one main thing and I'll be the master of it! There's a lot that I am capable of doing and plenty of things which I enjoy doing, so Lord, you help me make a decision so I don't spread myself thin doing 10, 000 things."

The Lord advised me that all that I had been doing was in preparation for ministry .And much of what I knew and experienced would be shared with others in due season. Let me first say that not all that you experience will make natural sense but by and by it will make spiritual sense and you will have a spiritual understanding.

It is important that as we seek the face of God we seek for spiritual wisdom and not operate in man's wisdom. For this reason, the Lord put people in place to give us words of wisdom as they apply to the spiritual things we will encounter and even those things we are commissioned by God to do.

I Cor 2:5-7 & 13

That your faith should not stand in the wisdom of men, but in the power of God.

Howbeit we speak wisdom among them that are perfect: yet not the wisdom of this world, not of the princes of this world, that come to nought.

But we speak the wisdom of God in a mystery, even the hidden wisdom, which God ordained before the world unto our glory.

Which things also we speak, not in the words which man's wisdom teacheth; comparing spiritual things with spiritual.

Man's wisdom tells us to take prayer out of schools. Man's wisdom also says that it's okay to have abortions. However, spiritual wisdom tells us that we ought to obey God rather than be pleasers of men.

WORD OF KNOWLEDGE

The Word of Knowledge explained simply is being led of the Spirit to tell someone something that you know through God. This can be past, present, or future. The Bible states that the Spirit knows all things and that Jesus is the Lord which is, which was, and which is to come (Rev 1:8). If you've been given this gift then expect to tell someone something they don't already know.

FYI: You will tell someone some things that have already been known to them at times. This is simply a form of confirmation to reassure that the Word given is from the Most High God.

Don't automatically go on the defense if a Prophet or Minister gives you a Word of Knowledge but it's something you already know and may have already come to pass. Understand that servants must be obedient to God and God will set multiple people in place sometimes to be sure His Word gets to you. That's just how much He loves us! When this happens, just take it as confirmation and keep going.

I attended a church service once and a prophetess began to speak a word of knowledge into my life along with some instructions. She said "you've got a lot on your mind, and you have a lot of responsibilities, but you've got to write! Get that stuff off of your mind and onto paper."

There was another service a few months following that my husband and I attended. There was a prophet there that spoke nearly the same thing into my life. He said "your responsibilities have you spread pretty thin, there is much that God is requiring of you and much that God is desiring to pour into you. However, there's just no room. God will not pour anymore until you download what you've already been given. You must write!" That wasn't the first or the last time I would hear those words.

The Spirit of God within me had already revealed this to me. So when it was told to me by the prophets I received it as a confirmation and any doubt or confusion that I had regarding the initial word that God had given me was removed. The Holy Ghost in me was in agreement with what was spoken and there was no inward conflict regarding authenticity.

Receiving is one thing; delivery is another. When delivering a word of knowledge to someone it is imperative that you stay focused on the mission and operate in obedience. Do not worry about how you will be received by the other party. Go forth with Holy boldness and authority knowing that otherwise the blood will be on your hands and you will be held accountable before God.

A few times the Lord used me to deliver a word of knowledge to someone along with a set of instructions and they were highly offended. They weren't so much offended by the instructions, but more so offended that it was revealed to me the things which I knew about them. Remember that God is a revealer of secrets.

II Cor 7:9-10

Now I rejoice, not that you were made sorry, but that ye sorrowed to repentance: For ye were made sorry after a godly manner, that ye might receive damage by us in nothing.

For godly sorrow worketh repentance to salvation not to be repented of: but the sorrow of the world worketh death.

Don't be concerned about offending someone with the Word. Plant the seeds in obedience as God wills and leave it there. We are not in the business of making friends, but in saving souls, and we most definitely don't negotiate with the devil! The Word is the Word and there is no compromising.

FAITH

What an awesome gift to bestow! Don't, however, confuse the gift of faith with natural faith. We are all given a measure of faith with the revelation of Jesus to believe unto salvation. But the gift of faith comes with Power and the ability to do all sorts of works and wonders through Christ which an ordinary allotment of faith does not afford us.

With the gift of faith many will be healed; broken hearts will be mended; blind eyes will see; deaf ears will hear; the lame will walk; the dead will live again! The list goes on for those possessing such a gift. There is no doubt, and those with this gift have a close relationship with Christ (or did at one point in time).

There was a question asked of me once, "why does the bible say to desire prophesy more than the other gifts when the gift of faith gives you the ability to do seemingly so much more in the kingdom of God?" With faith all things are possible. And to answer that question as someone with spiritual understanding is to say that they are co-related and could even be considered a gift within a gift.

Faith is the author of prophecy. Jesus is faith. He tells us in the book of Revelation that He is the God which is, which was, and which is to come. Sound familiar? So then faith, too, is, was, and is to come. So with these gifts being practically one in the same (seeing you can't really have one without the other). You should covet the gift of faith just as much as prophecy.

The difference between the initial measure of faith that God has given us and the gift of faith is that the gift of faith doesn't require activation or building up. Our natural faith is built as we draw nearer to God and continue to seek His faith. However, with the gift of faith this is not necessary. You don't need practice or testimony to operate therein.

I've witnessed the lifestyle of a few people with this gift. They are unstoppable and the sky is the limit with what they can do. However, that doesn't necessarily mean that they have a close relationship with Christ (though they should). Remember gifts are without repentance. Though one may possess this gift to "make things happen", I encourage you to have a passionate pursuit of the face of God. This will keep you anchored in Him and you will be most effective in battle for Christ.

THE GIFT OF HEALING

The gift of healing operates similar to the above mentioned gift of faith. Healing covers several aspects in a person's life and goes far beyond sickness and disease. Sometimes there is a need for emotional healing and this can accompany forgiveness.

In some cases, men and women may need to be healed of a certain mindset and they experience transformation of the mind and old ways of thinking. Keep in mind that healing takes place in the natural sense as well as in the spiritual sense (we'll get the details in a later chapter).

Someone can be healed from a word of wisdom, word of knowledge, a preached word, or even laying on of hands to name a few. When one is given this gift the Lord will train you on how to operate in such a gift. Though you may be used by God to heal using all sorts of methods, in many cases you will find that the Lord may use one "main" or consistent way to have you operate in your gift. I myself have the gift of healing and the "main" way in which the Lord has me to function in my gift is through laying on of hands.

The thing to understand with the gift of healing as it refers to ailments in the natural sense is that there are three main sources that stem from the need of healing. Some things are put on by God, some by the enemy, and others simply for the sake of the operation of God's Spirit. All-in-all that God will be glorified. Before healing can come about, one must get to the "root" cause of why healing needs to take place in one's life or family.

REBELLION AND SIN

Rebellion and sin are reasons why someone may be stricken with sickness. When presented with the Word of God it is our choice if we will take heed and walk in obedience. When you decide to be of the world, the Lord allows the prince of the air and the father of the children of disobedience to have rule over certain aspects of your life. Diseases and infirmities often become a factor such as Cancer, AIDS, Diabetes, and the like. The Lord may allow such because of sins such as adultery, smoking, or something seeming small such as not eating right. Your flesh must be placed under subjection. Once there is full surrender then there can be full healing. In many instances deliverance must precede the healing process.

CURSES

Another root cause of why someone may need healing is due to curses. One of the most common type of curse is a generational curse. You can trickle a generational curse, however, most often have an origination from several years prior or even generations prior. The curses stem from actions of ancestors and regardless of the origination, they can end with you and your decision to choose Jesus. For healing to take place the instruction may be fasting, prayer and supplication, praise and worship or even all of the above.

In my own life there was a particular occasion I had gone on a fast to get results regarding my personal walk with

Christ. It was my desire to press to the next spiritual level and I found myself hindered in my praise and worship. The Lord revealed to me that I had the curse of worship over my life. He went on to tell me that it was due to no fault of my own by originated many generation prior. I was told that in order to get the results I desired and to break the curse, I needed to do a full blown, all-out praise and worship like I had never done before. So I went into an all-out praise "explosion" and didn't stop until I dropped. The curse was broken. Deliverance took place, opening doors for healing, and continued spiritual growth in Christ. This is a prime example of a thing being put on by God and required intervention of God for complete healing.

CIRCUMSTANCE

Heb 12:1

> *Wherefore seeing we also are compassed with so great a cloud of witnesses, let us lay aside every weight that so easily beset us, and let us run with patience the race that is set before us,*

There are some cases where there is a healing due to circumstances and life's trials of faith. There was a time I counseled someone who couldn't begin to truly flourish in Christ because of the death of a close family member who seemed to be the only positive re-enforcement in their life. They knew Jesus to be their personal Lord and Savior but harbored anger and bitterness. They hungered for understanding of why God would allow such a tragedy to occur. After being given words of wisdom and words of knowledge, fertilized with the Power of the Holy Ghost;

mending of a broken heart took place which brought about healing and joy in their relationship with Christ.

John 9:2

> And His disciples asked him, saying, Master, who did sin, this man, or his parents, that he was born blind?
>
> Jesus answered, Neither hath this man sinned, nor his parents: but that the works of God should be made manifest in him.

No matter how well you strive to be obedient to the will and purpose of Christ circumstances and situations will come about. Be confident knowing that some suffering is for righteousness sake and that some things God will allow for the operations of His spirit to be manifest in you. Sometimes people simply need to see that Jesus is real and that in Him no one is broken beyond repair.

EMOTIONS

It's imperative that you decrease and allow the Holy Ghost to reveal to you the things you can control and give you the wisdom to know what you should let go of and allow the Lord to handle. I can reflect back to a time when I was stricken with sickness and on the first day as I was in prayer the Lord came to me. He stated that I had be stricken with sickness in my body and that it originated because of worry. I continued to worry about certain family members that I was praying for and because I kept picking the thing up and interfering with something that should have been left at the alter I was inflicted with sickness. This sickness was put on by God. The instruction from God was that He would heal me if I praised Him. Not only did the situation cause me to worry but it interfered with my joy. I was obedient and praised God. Joy was restored and I fully relinquished my authority over the situation and gave it completely to God.

Lay aside every weight and allow the Holy Ghost to be your comforter through situations you are faced with. Don't allow emotions to create wounds that will require God to intervene and heal. Again, the Spirit of God is not emotional but operates in Power, love and soundness of mind.

If you are the vessel that God is using to heal others then make sure you have the authority to heal that person. Hearken unto the voice of God so that you're operating within His will. Some ailments put on by God must be removed in His perfect timing lest you take on another man's sin and bring chastisement upon yourself. Ask yourself "Is it God or is it man? Do I want them healed, or does God want them healed?"

MIRACLES

The gift of miracles is a mind blowing and incredible gift to possess. What is a miracle? A miracle is an unnatural occurrence in which something is done and there can be no credit given to an earthly entity and cannot be scientifically be explained.

An example of a miracle being performed is when Moses was used by God to part the Red Sea and God allowed the children of Israel to walk through on dry land. This cannot be scientifically explained away. Another miracle you may consider is being used to have an amputated limb grow back before your very eyes. The Lord on numerous occasions raised the dead as well. God gets all of the glory in these situations.

For some reason miracles have often been associated with positive attributes. These often include prosperity, wealth, or success. However, miracles are also associated with the wrath of God, as well as devastation and death.

Faith is not required to activate a miracle. God uses miracles for the non-believer to be transformed into believers. He used working of miracles to build the faith of His children. The Lord also performed miracles as an operation of His Spirit upon the earth and to carryout prophecy.

An example of God working miracles for the non-believers and as faith builders was in the Old Testament when God chose Moses to lead the children of Israel. Though Moses had a relationship with God, the people still needed to be introduced to God as their Savior and Deliverer. This is shown often as the Word stated that God was the God of their fathers Abraham, Isaac, and Jacob. Yet God desired to establish a relationship with the children of Israel and He used several miracles to do so!

Besides parting the Red Sea, the Lord also led the children of Israel in a cloud by day and fire by night. He also used Moses on numerous occasions while in the wilderness to provide food and water for His people. These works allowed for the Children of Israel to build a faith and recognize that He was in fact the Most High God.

A New Testament miracle was performed when Jesus bid Peter to walk on water. This was used not only to build the faith or Peter to also build the faith of the other disciples which were there to witness such a work. The disciples already knew Jesus but the working of such a miracle produced a transformed mindset that not only were they followers of Christ but with the belief and Power of God, they too, could do the works of Christ and together could do a greater work.

Other times the Lord performed miracles in necessity for the operation His Spirit. This lets people know that no matter whether they choose to follow Him or surrender to His will, He is still God. His Word is true and will not return void. There were times where miracles were performed as a call for a national repentance due to disobedience, and on occasion people were used as an example to others. God performed miracles through changes in weather, using animals, and even such wonders as sinkholes across the United States and abroad.

Num 16:30

> But if the Lord make a new thing, and the earth open her mouth, and swallow them up, with all that appertain unto them, and they go down quick into the pit; then ye shall understand that these men have provoked the Lord.

When Korah gathered the children of Israel against Moses and Aaron, God's wrath kindled and to make them as an example to the rest of God's people he performed a miracle in which the earth swallowed them up. This is an operation of the Spirit of God and was used to re-establish fear and reverence among them.

I Kings 13:24-26

> And when he was gone, a lion met him by the way, and slew him: and his carcase was cast in the way, and the ass stood by it, the lion also stood by the carcase.
>
> And, behold, men passed by, and saw the carcase cast in the way, and the lion standing by the carcase: and they came and told it in the city where the old prophet delt.
>
> And when the prophet that brought him back from the way heard thereof, he said, It is the man of God, who was disobedient unto the Word of the

Lord: therefore the Lord hath delivered him unto the lion, which hath torn him, and slain him, according to the Word of the Lord, which He spake unto him.

Though many examples of working of miracles were done directly by God, we now have access to His Spirit and it is important to use this gift for the building up of the kingdom of God and to operate according to His will. Many have started small, with humble beginnings, being trained by God and somewhere along the lines have strayed from the faith. For reasons of disobedience we often see the operation of the Spirit of God to bring about repentance and restore order among His people.

As close as Moses was to God, frustration along with disobedience was the cause of him missing the opportunity to get to the Promised Land. God desired to use him to work a miracle before the children of Israel. He was instructed to speak to the rock, instead, in frustration and agitation with the people, he smote the rock. For his disobedience he paid a life changing consequence. His life was cut short just prior to getting to the land that God had promised. Don't sacrifice your reward of eternal life because of misuse of the gift God has given or because of disobedience.

Every day that the sun rises and sets is a miracle. The glisten of the moon is a miracle. The sparkle of the stars is a miracle. Who can understand? Who can rationalize?

At the beginning of the calendar year 2013, the Lord proclaimed by the mouth of the prophets that it would be a year of miracles and it was, indeed. We saw record breaking weather events all over the world that have never been recorded in history. We saw things like sink holes swallow up men and their homes. We also saw snow fall in places that never received snow in all of history.

One thing about miracles is that they can either be negative or positive. When many hear of a miracle, they may think of an unexpected monetary deposit in a bank account or someone being brought back to life from the dead. One hesitates to mention the operation of God's Spirit in wrath and fury upon the disobedient.

PROPHESY

The gift of prophesy is another spiritual gift that is distributed by the Spirit of God. This gift should be desired above all other gifts (1 Cor 14:1). Don't confuse the gift of prophesy with being a prophet. You can have the gift of prophesy but that doesn't entitle you to start calling yourself a prophet or prophetess.

The gift of prophesy is used for the edification of the saints of God. Again, I remind you that prophesy is past, present, and future as was mentioned with the word of knowledge earlier.

This gift allows one to have vision to see and speak of the things to come. This gift may also lead one to speak a word of wisdom, or word of knowledge, and understanding of things foretold. Oftentimes, the gift of prophesy will be used as a form of instruction given by God to be sure that the people and saints of God have a Sheppard and are fed according to the will of God. You will find many Pastors and Apostles with this gift because it is a spiritual necessity for leading the flock.

The Bible mentions that the Spirit of the Prophets is subject to the Prophets. Though not all who have the prophetic gift are prophets, they are still operating in the same spirit and therefore this spirit gives confirmation. This too is when we apply the scripture where it is written: "let two prophesy and let another be the judge."

As one having the prophetic gift, it is imperative that you know your role in such a gift. The prophetic gift when in operation appropriately and most effectively has an understanding of the lord's flow and timing. There's an old saying, "there's a wrong way to do right."

Be sure to operate in sync with the Spirit of God. The Holy Ghost doesn't move against itself. Your gift will make room for you. God will not lead you to interrupt a service that is flowing by His spirit to deliver a Word. There is and will be an ordained time for the prophetic gift within you to flourish; whether it be during the praise and worship service, alter call, or any other time that the Lord ordains.

You must oftentimes ask yourself the questions, "Is it God? Or is it man?" With the prophetic gift comes the ability to operate in Gods authority. With such authority is the power to speak things into the life of others, whether it be positive or negative; true or false.

It is understandable that you may want certain things to manifest for other people, but at no time do you force a word. Again, the Spirit speaks what He sees and what He hears. If you didn't see it or you didn't hear it, don't speak it! That's it! That's all! The same God that built you up is the same God that will tear you down. Speak His Word. Do not add or subtract from it lest you find yourself hearing the words "depart from me you workers of iniquity."

With the prophetic operation of the Spirit a person has the ability to speak things into the lives of others. This is where you notice false apostles, false prophets and the like. With every gift there are demonic forces assigned to war with those having these diverse gifts.

In particular, the prophetic draws witches, warlocks, sorcerers, workers of iniquity, and all other spiritual wickedness in high places. Now, don't get me wrong. You can work witchcraft (rebellion) and still belong to God. However, being an actual witch or warlock; you've gone through that door to the point of no return (spoken of in later chapters). You're no longer on the Lord's side and for some folks, they never were on the Lord's side and never will be.

I made mention also of spiritual wickedness in high places. What does that really mean? Have you ever noticed in the scriptures when there is mention of worship or sacrifice that it is always done in a place by people of great power or authority (i.e. High priests, Kings)?

Abraham went yonder to the high place to sacrifice his son Isaac to the Lord (Gen 22:5). Once the Lord saw his heart and his desire to be obedient He intervened and provided a ram in the thickets. However, not all sacrifices in high places were sacrifices in righteousness and holiness. Some sacrifices were done in wickedness by kings and by many of the children of Israel. They sacrificed to idol gods in high places doing wickedness in the sight of God.

The significance that I want to point out is that these people who made these sacrifices were not of lowly estate. They were chosen people of a "royal priesthood". They were those who were on higher spiritual levels of wisdom, knowledge, understanding, and even favor with God.

Even today we find the same great men and women of God who have been shown favor to operate in certain positions. These positions include apostleship, pastorship, presidency, and other roles of great influence.

When placed in high spiritual positions, the enemy comes in do his job which is to temp us. Will you take the bait? He tries to tempt us to rebel against God, speaking lies in hypocrisy, seducing the people of God and even convincing them to divine for money.

There are many who will approach you with desires to pervert the gospel. Avoid them at all cost. Be sure your sacrifices are for righteousness and holiness. Some think of sacrifice as a way of the past because it is a part of the old covenant. The ceremonies took place in the natural realm and they sacrificed animals to be cleansed of sins. The wicked children of disobedience sacrificed animals unto idols and devils. However, now we know that everything is spiritual. So everything manifest in the natural realm must first be present in spirit.

I've experienced warfare in the Spirit with a number of false prophets. Because I was not obedient to their personal desires they took it upon themselves to call upon the Spirit of the lion and of the bear to devour me in the Spirit. However, in the natural realm it would seem as if everything is fine. The warfare against these lions and bears was fierce and it required the diligence on my part and my husband to diligently seek the face of God through our prayers, reading our Word, and most importantly through our praise. The enemy is relentless and if you take down your defenses you will fall.

Those who operate in the prophetic, I urge you to take this gifting/calling seriously. You cannot play around with these spirits that you encounter in the spiritual realm. Warfare is real and you will be held accountable. The wages of sin is death.

DISCERNING OF SPIRITS

Discerning of spirits in another gift distributed by the Holy Ghost. This gift goes beyond the day to day discernment that is given us to discern the difference between right and wrong and the like. Discerning of spirits is a treasure for a warrior in God's army. This gift allows one to know the name of the spirit, principality, or demonic force in operation.

When one has the Holy Ghost they utilize their power and authority to speak directly to problems and circumstances occurring in one's life. We pray fervently to cast out devils that a person may be oppressed or suppressed by. However, some are entangled by more than one spirit or demonic force and to make for speedy deliverance the Lord allows for one having the discerning of spirits to call the demonic force by name and it is then that is cast out.

Daniel 10:13

> *But the Prince of the kingdom of Persia withstood me one and twenty days: but, lo, Michael one of the chief princes, came to help me; and I remained there with the kings of Persia.*

Demonic forces don't just want to occupy people but they have command over certain areas, countries, cities, and states. So looking at spiritual warfare with a broader scope, the discerner of spirits has knowledge of such powers, principalities, and demonic forces in operation over provinces and towns and can therefore aid in the spiritual necessity of God's people on a whole and what is required for a full blown revival or deliverance.

I've found that with this gift many become agitated easily when subject to lots of demonic forces, especially those who are unlearned and really don't understand what's going on spiritually. You may often experience headaches and even troubles with your bowls. It is important to recognize the spiritual surroundings and the company that you keep. Be sure to continue to guard your anointing and avoid high traffic areas where demonic forces are sure to be present such as shopping malls, concerts, shows, clubs, and the like.

Let me tell you of time my husband and I purchased our second home. While going through the closing process, the realtor that represented the sellers had disclosed to us that there was no problem with the home but that the owners had gone through a divorce.

Well, after the closing, my husband and I went to the property to check things out so we could get started on the move. All the utilities were on and the last thing to do was bless the house. We started downstairs in the garage, praying and applying the oil to the walls. Then we worked our way into the kitchen. After the kitchen, we made our way into the basement. Initially, I discerned something wasn't right but it didn't come to me right away. I continued to walk through with the oil and was encountered by two demonic forces. The first named murder and the second named kill. I began to rebuke the spirits but these spirits were not passersby. These demonic forces had begun to make a sanctuary in the basement. They tried to take us out right then but thank God for the blood of Jesus. They were cast out and we continued to move upstairs to the bedrooms. Once we arrived in the master bedroom I heard footsteps in the room. It wasn't natural; it was spiritual. I couldn't pinpoint where they were coming from. Then we called out, "spirit of darkness, what is your name?" The spirit responded:

"Hidden, for I am a hidden spirit."

Then again, we pleased the blood of Christ and that spirit was cast out as well.

Naturally, the Lord gives us a measure of discernment to recognize whether something is wrong or uncomfortable. However, through the gift of the Holy Ghost we have access to the gift of discerning of spirits. This affords us the ability to know exactly what we are fighting against and allows for preparation of the appropriate weapons to go forth and conquer.

There was a time where I had to find this out the hard way. I was so zealous about spreading the Word and just trying to be of some use to Lord by going "outside the walls" of the church. So I said what I would do was sign up with two of the local prisons and bring copies of my book and minister from time to time. Of course, I fasted and prayed. The Spirit and His prophet told me not to go. I chucked it up to the enemy trying to interfere with the Lord's work. However, this is not something that the Lord had ordained or commissioned me to do. Needless to say, when I went in the work of the Lord was done. The group received my book and the ministering thereof seemingly with open arms but the encounter with the demonic forces left me so spiritually drained that day that I was no earthly good to anyone else the rest of that week for healing (by laying on of hands which is my main gift). It took approximately three and half days to rebuild my anointing through yet another fast and high, high praise. I believe it wouldn't have taken that long if I wasn't out of order. God has anointed people to perform certain operations of the Spirit as I have mentioned before. Know where you belong and master it, zeal or not! I should have been able to discern that those spirits in that prison were not for me to be dealing with. I returned home and immediately my stomach was upset. In between running back and forth to the bathroom I was trying to pray, and repent, and praise, and you name it. It may be funny now, but at the time I cried out to God like it was my last chance. This is another reason why it is so important to be led by His Spirit regardless if you think, "you're spreading the word...so God won't mind". Yes, He will mind! Be sure to discern what is the Spirit of God and what is flesh!

DIVERSE KINDS OF TONGUES

Having the gift of diverse kinds of tongues allows for the possessor to speak in different languages whether Spanish, English, German, French, Chinese, Japanese, and the like. This ability is given so that Jesus can effectively deliver a message or instruction to His people.

Diversity of tongues is also given as a sign to the believer. It is the evidence of the Spirit of God as shown in Acts 2:8 and Acts 2:11. The people were amazed and believed even the more because of the wonderful works of God spoken in their own tongue.

Most often those who have been distributed this gift has and will also be give the gift of interpretation of tongues (mentioned later). It is necessary to have the interpretation of tongues so that all are edified and no spectators or standers by are left in confusion.

Those using these tongues are often used by God to speak to crowds of people and God leaves very few, if any, spectators that are left in need of interpretation.

Though one may have this gift, it is important to be led of the Spirit when initiating its use. Sometimes when being used in a gift such as this, it is normal to be excited. Not just excited about the gift itself, but to be eager in zeal to be used by God. Don't have unlearned zeal (zeal without knowledge). The gift will make room for itself.

I remember shopping for groceries on one occasion. In the midst of one of the isles I spotted a woman who was speaking in tongues loud enough to be heard in the other isles, for what? Had she gone mad? Yep. Keep the flesh under subjection and surely God will use you more than you ever could have imagined.

INTERPRETATION OF TONGUES

The interpretation of tongues is a gift distributed by the Holy Ghost so that one may translate the communications of unknown tongues and other tongues or languages. Interpretation of diverse tongues is common among Apostles and Prophets but can be distributed to others having the Holy Ghost as well. The purpose of such a gift is so that hearers of such tongues will not be left in confusion but that all will be edified in Christ.

The gift of interpretation of tongues also comes with the ability to decipher between godly and ungodly tongues. Because we are in constant spiritual warfare, one will be confronted by deceiving spirits and spirits that mock the Holy Ghost. Speaking in an unknown tongue is our evidence that we have the Holy Ghost. Christians know this and the enemy knows this as well. This is evidence of our power and authority.

Satan tries to penetrate our spiritual lines of defense. To be successful in such an endeavor, one requires access through a weak vessel or by sending a mole that will mock and mimic the power of God in order to be perceived as one of our own. With such access the enemy gains an inside track to our behind the scenes operations and administrations. Such access can render our operations temporarily ineffective. Again, this is why there is a great necessity to know them that labor among us and to try the spirits by the spirit. This gift helps weed out the real from the fake.

I believe this is why this gift is so prominent among the Prophets. Knowing that the spirit of the prophets is subject to the prophets; allows them be the judge of what is true and maintain order within the church.

I had a dream once where I was overseas in a place where it seemed to be dry and desert-like. I was in a ministering capacity and there were people with children outside. Many were being healed, set free, and even receiving the Holy Ghost. Then all of a sudden another minister comes up to me leading a young boy by the hand and he said, "Look, Pastor, He speaks in tongues". Immediately I began to plead the blood for the boy was not of an accountable age, and I said to the minister, "these tongues are not of God". Then that dream came to an end.

I believe the Lord has allowed for the operation of this very gift so that His people are able to decipher what is real and what is not. This is also why He is called the Spirit of Truth. We must be able to recognize when God's work is truly being done and that we are not in the midst of a bunch of mockery and placing ourselves in positions to have our virtue drained and there is no edification of His people in the process.

Although one may possess the gift of interpretation, that doesn't mean that it must always be put to use. Just as a preacher doesn't go preaching 24/7 and the prophets don't just go around speaking the mysteries of God, accept it be at the appointed time. Because the Spirit of God knows all things and is a revealer of secrets, we still must equally exercise discretion. Your gift can be at work internally (especially when you've killed flesh and you're walking in the Spirit). However, just like a lamp plugged in, but not clicked on is how you should be also. Know God's time and order. Don't reveal unless prompted or ordered by the Spirit to do so.

CHAPTER IV

CALLINGS

WHAT DID YOU CALL ME?

CALLINGS

MATT 22:14

For many are called but few are chosen.

It's one thing for God to call you. It is another for one to completely surrender and answer the call to become one of the chosen. There are different degrees and levels of the callings of God. The Lord has called us into righteousness and Holiness. He has also called us to be saints, disciples, and even called many into ministry.

Some confuse the callings of God with gifts, appointments, and even offices. First, let me state that a call can only be made by God and there is not a guarantee that you will be chosen. Whereas gifts are distributed as God wills and are without repentance and unto death. Appointments and offices can be assignments given by man and most are not intended to be permanent as with many callings; they are.

I Peter 2:9

> *But ye are a chosen generation, a royal priesthood, an Holy nation, a peculiar people; that ye should shew forth the praises of him who hath called you out of darkness into His marvelous light:*

THE NEW CONVERT

One of the first calls that God makes is the call out of the world of darkness into the righteousness of Christ. With the acceptance of this call comes the gift of God unto salvation and eternal life. At this point, one is a new convert. One is then taught about the expectations of God and the new life they will live. This is where you begin to seek God for the indwelling of the Holy Ghost. The Holy Ghost is our best teacher.

I Cor 1:2

> *Unto the church of God which is at Corinth, to them that are sanctified in Christ, called to be saints, with all that in every place call upon the name of Jesus Christ our Lord both theirs and ours:*

THE SAINT

Another call mentioned in the Word is the call to be a saint. Not everyone is considered to be a saint, which is contrary to popular belief. The Apostle Paul reminds us that the call to be a saint can only be accepted by those that are sanctified and set apart from the cares of the world, walking in holiness and righteousness. Saints of God are not just hearers of the Word but doers also.

Matt 10:1

> *And when He had called unto Him His twelve disciples, He gave them power against spirits, to cast them out, and to heal all manner of sickness and all manner of disease.*

THE DISCIPLE

So we recognize that a disciple goes beyond being merely a saint. Disciples are true and faithful followers of Christ. They are not only obedient to the Word of God but have the power of the Holy Ghost and have been chosen or commissioned to do the works that Christ did.

The commission of the disciples was to go forth and to heal all manner of sickness, clean lepers, raise the dead, cast out devils, and to preach the gospel of Christ (Matt 10:8).

To function and operate as a disciple of Christ one needs to have thorough knowledge and understanding of the Word of God which is necessary for the warfare with casting out devils. One must also possess high levels of faith without wavering, compromise, and having holy boldness and confidence. Those called to such a role must be seasoned and walk in a close relationship with Christ. You must not only be called but be chosen and sent by God for such missions.

Eph 4:11-12

> And He gave some, Apostles; and some, Prophets; and some Evangelists; and some Pastors and teachers;

> For the perfecting of the saints, for the work of the ministry, for the edifying of the body of Christ:

Some are called to higher spiritual levels in Christ and are set aside for the work in the ministry and to edify the saints of God. The ministerial callings are a part of what many may call a five-fold ministry.

THE TEACHER

There are many that are called and chosen by God to be teachers. One may be called a teacher but many may also be appointed to other temporary assignments or offices addressed later in the chapter.

Those who are called to teach the children of God usually have the compassion and patience necessary for such a role. The teachers are seasoned in the Word but are gifted with the ability to effectively communicate their understanding of the Word to others.

The call of a Pastor is very similar to that of a teacher. Pastors are teachers but not all teachers are pastors. It is the pastors' responsibility to Sheppard the children of God. Beyond teaching, they are nurturers making sure that the flock receives the Word and applies it properly. They lead and guide the flock in the direction the Lord wants them to go. Metaphorically speaking, one could consider a pastor to be a farmer. They plant seeds, water seeds, fertilizing as needed so that the harvest of God is righteous and plentiful.

THE EVANGELIST

One called to be an evangelist has a unique calling. After close studies of the Word of God you'll find that the evangelists of the early church were not commissioned by God to preach within the local church but ventured outside the local providences to outside towns, cities, and countries proclaiming and declaring the gospel of Jesus Christ to them that were lost.

You can consider this operation of the Spirit to be an outreach mission. I've seen a number of people called to be Evangelists operate outside of their calling and stick within their local church and they seemed rather boring. There is no true edification because they are out of order. Evangelists are fire starters and are often appointed preachers. They flourish when they are breaking beyond church walls and going among the lost and the poor, winning souls for Christ.

Know who God has called you to be. Don't let anyone else tell you who you are. Break out of your comfort zone. Keep your bags packed and don't be afraid to go where no man has gone before. For the well aren't the ones in need of a physician....Break new ground, lay new foundations and be the undertakers for the devil!

THE PROPHET/PROPHETESS

Prophets are commissioned by God to speak the past, present, and future happenings and the such to the people and in areas the Lord may instruct. Please be reminded not to confuse the prophetic call with the prophetic gift. One may co-relate a prophetic call as a career; that's their main operation. Whereas one possessing the prophetic gift would use it more as a resource necessary to fulfill the duties and responsibilities effectively in another call, for example, as a pastor or apostle. The prophet speaks the Word in most cases to teach, reprove, correct, or even give warning. You'll find that prophets are not nurturers and caretakers. It is not their responsibility to groom the Word or be sure it is received. They speak what thus saith the Lord and they leave it there (unlike a pastor or teacher).

One of the most important things to understand while operating as a prophet is the need to operate in decency and in order. The scripture in Ephesian 4:4 tells us that God gave first the Apostles and secondarily prophets. To give an understanding is that prophets come second as the "eyes" or "seers" of the body so there is direction to a vision in Christ. Don't confuse this with being the "head" of the body. At no time do you present yourself above the head or Sheppard.

I must also stress the importance of confidentiality. Keep in mind that you are ONLY the vessel that the Lord is using to deliver a message to His people. Oftentimes, I've witnessed lots of mess once a prophet/prophetess had gotten back into the flesh. They may use information that has been revealed through the prophetic against someone. As saints, we are not to hold information over someone's head or attempt to use what we know to disrupt the body by gossiping or releasing information to others for instigation or agitation. I've heard things like "that's why God told you that you need to surrender," or "that's the real reason your blessings are being delayed." Do not fall into the hands of angry God. Again, I say to speak the Word and leave it there.

If you ever feel that another person may benefit from knowledge that was revealed through you, please ask permission to release the information and cover the identities of all parties until permission has been given. Just because you think it should be done, doesn't make it righteous. Don't operate on your own accord and authority. Move by the Spirit and avoid friendly fire and creating unnecessary storms within the body. Be good stewards of the information that God shares with you. Remember that God reveals His secrets for the uplifting of His kingdom and for tearing down the kingdom of Satan.

A true prophet of the Most High God knows their place and role on the battlefield for Christ and learns to "master" that role. To "master" your warfare, you must be proficient in your calling. Do not add any additional responsibilities to your place in this role unless appointed to do so.

THE APOSTLE

The call of the Apostle in the five-fold ministry is the highest ministerial call there is. This call should not be taken lightly. Many have given themselves this title that were neither called nor sent. This call is reserved by God for the Most Holy, humble, and faithful of all servants. The Apostle should do the work of an evangelist, pastor, teacher, and should have the prophetic gift. Apostles were authorized to appoint Elders and other officers as the Lord has instructed, to include officiating ordinations of leaders and others chosen by God to do a work. The Apostle is a pioneer. This means they are charged with laying the ground-breaking foundation of Christ where is had never been laid before. They set the standard for others to follow. It was the Apostle Paul who instructed us to follow after him as he follows Christ. The Apostle is commissioned to war with principalities, rulers of darkness, and spiritual wickedness in high places. There are demons specifically assigned to war with those called to this position (as with others) and for this reason many are strongly warned not to self-promote. Let God call and qualify you. Operate in your appropriate call and appointments.

I was approached by someone who stated to me that all it means to be an Apostle is that it means to be sent by God. That is absolutely incorrect. A true prophet is sent. A true pastor is sent. We all can't be apostles. I was told that as long as they had a church prophet, a church evangelist, and a pastor or teacher under them, that they had the five-fold. No! The complete five-fold is within the Apostle. The Apostle of the Most High God doesn't piggy-back off the anointing of their people. The oil runs from top to bottom. Don't be an anointing sucker. Be who you are called to be. An Apostle that is operating like this and not having the true five-fold within themselves are destined to fall due to demonic forces they are not equipped to fight. They are also operating on unstable foundations, really standing on the foundations of others. With one bad storm, they will come tumbling down.

I must also stress again that the apostle is a foundation builder. Nowadays, many are seeking a microwave ministry. No one wants to build from the ground up and many who see someone building don't want to be a part of a ministry in the building stages. They wait and wait until everything is built and establish. How lazy! Building from the ground requires hard work and there are no shortcuts. I've come across many Apostles who go hunting and looking for ministries who are already established desiring to take over as the Head. Is it God or is it man? Bishops are appointed, but the Apostles are the master builders. I've found many Apostles taking credit for the building of foundations that weren't laid by them.

Romans 15:20-21

> *Yea, so have I strived to preach the gospel, not where Christ was named, lest I should build upon another man's foundation:*
>
> *But as it is written, to whom he was not spoken of, they shall see: and they that have not heard shall understand.*

Please do not allow the flesh to dictate your calling. Move by the Spirit and know the voice of God. Again, I say if it's not God then its flesh. Feed the flesh and the flesh will live. Starve the flesh and the flesh will die. Seek the face of God and do not worry about the people and their faces.

THE APPOINTMENTS

Num 4:19

> *But thus do unto them, that they may live, and not die, when they approach unto the most holy things: Aaron and his sons shall go in, and appoint them every one to his service and to his burden:*

Oftentimes, the difference between callings and appointment can be confusing. It is important to know your identity so that you can effectively execute the responsibility and duties that accompany it. There may be number of missions that one is called to carry out but there is only one five-fold ministerial calling.

Of course, there are elevations at the time appointed by God. But, there is no such thing as a Prophet Pastor or a Prophet Evangelist. That is just one example. I have also seen people fall into comfort zones and be okay with the idea that they have been a deacon/deaconess for years. Yes, that may be all well and good but, what were they actually CALLED to do. Deacon is an appointment and as the above scripture states, an additional burden; not the calling. Know the difference. It's important that those in leadership do not become authority abusers with the Holy Ghost but be sure to allow God's people to stir up the gifts of God within them and go beyond just the helps and missionary responsibilities, if they are indeed called to do more.

THE DEACON

1 Tim 3:10

> *And let those also first be proved; then let them use the office of a deacon, being found blameless.*

As mentioned earlier, there are some appointments made by God, and other appointments made by man. The Deacon is one of those appointments that the Lord allows man to make as necessary for the edification of the body. The Spirit of God should play a role in the decision-making process. However, it is not necessary for a prophet of the Most High to be sent to seal or ordain one appointed to this office. The roles and duties of a Deacon may vary depending upon the type of operation and the needs of that particular operation necessary to function. One may take offerings, clean the church, order/keep track of supplies, etc. They are responsible for hospitality operations and other helps and missions as assigned.

THE BISHOP

The bible tells us that those desiring the office of Bishop desire a good work. The bishop is considered a calling by many but biblically considered an appointment based on the idea that one can aspire to fill such an office. The office of a Bishop is usually held by an elder or one seasoned in the Word. The bishop was responsible for overseeing the flocks of God, protecting them from the enemy, being apt to teach and exhort, as necessary. In my experience, bishops were usually appointed over a flock that was founded (foundation was laid) by an Apostle. Especially understanding that the Apostle establishes the foundations of Christ as master builders and then moves on. Who cares for the flock that the Apostle builds up? The bishop. Is this always the case? No. However, it is a very accurate example of what one may see.

THE ELDER

Acts 14:23

> *And when they had ordained them elders in every church, and had prayed with fasting, they commended them to the Lord, on whom they believed.*

The Elders are the pillars of the church. As an elder you are expected to be seasoned in the Word of God. Elders should possess the ability to get a prayer through and be able to lay hands on the sick that they may recover. The bible tells us that if there be any sick among you let them call upon the Elders. It is the responsibility of an Elder to assist with maintaining order within the church and at times bear the infirmities of the weak.

Someone asked me what the difference between an Elder and a Bishop was. I will say that there is one main difference. The Elders are judges. They have been appointed by to assist Kings, Apostles, and other leadership to judge nations. Moses is used to set this example for us when his father-in-law Jethro advises him to appoint Elders to help judge the situations of the people so that he was not overwhelmed. They must be able to render righteous judgment and measure things according to the Word of God with objectivity.

The Elders are the elite in Christ and should therefore act accordingly. Speaking from a warfare perspective; the Elders are often responsible for covert missions and operations. They are the watch towers of our souls and can look down from on High and see those in distress, wounded, and even those who have become prisoners of war. The covert mission is to assess the battleground, create strategic plans of action, and rescue the lost bringing them to safety.

Ezekiel 34:16

> *I will seek that which was lost, and bring again that which was driven away, and will bind up that which was broken, and will strengthen that which was sick......*

At no time should an Elder be missing in action or AWOL (absent without leave), though, oftentimes they are. As the Elite, the Elders have close relationships with Christ and should therefore be able to make decisions even without instructions or "orders". Avoid being a confirmation junkie. If you move and operate in the Spirit then it's Christ and He doesn't need to be confirmed.

Naturally, there are other appointments and operations of helps from faith to faith as the Lord leads. However, these are the main operations as mentioned in the Word of God. The Lord gives us choices as far as what we desire for assistance in ministry and because of this, we also decide the ADDITIONAL rights and responsibilities that seem fit for such roles. I say additional because this doesn't alleviate our original responsibilities as disciples of the Most High.

CHAPTER V

HOW DO I CONDUCT MYSELF?

ADMINISTRATIONS AND OPERATIONS

1 COR 12:5

And there are differences of administrations, but the same Lord.

The enemy has an agenda to steal, kill, and destroy. He operates in several shapes, fashions, forms and dimensions in order to carry out this agenda. The Lord also has a mission and uses several shapes, fashions, forms, and dimensions to accomplish such missions.

We know that God has several goals and missions which goes far beyond the gift of salvation. We as a people deal with diverse spirits, personalities, cultures, and ways of life. Not only do we have diverse needs, but we have diverse ways of learning. Because of this, the Spirit of God has diversified administrations and operations.

An operation of the Spirit is the process in which the Lord uses to build foundations and prepare people or ministries to function. The process the Lord takes to operate within one ministry may be different from the process the Lord takes to operate in another ministry. Several factors play a role.

Some ministries are solely teaching ministries, while others teach, preach, and even train future ministers. There are other ministries that are called "powerhouses" where one may go to get spiritual "refueling". In this case, you may find that there is awesome high praise and worship experiences but not necessarily all of the spiritual bread and water ultimately required for full maturity. For this reason, we can have Apostolic churches, Holiness churches, Pentecostal and so forth. The Spirit operates through these members of the one body, all in all.

While the Spirit continues to operate, certain administrations are necessary. God is a God that does things decently and in order. He records all things in heaven. So, as it is in the Spirit, it is also in the natural realm.

Some of the administrative duties include keeping record of the operations within the church or the body of Christ. Some of these duties include licensing and ordinations to name a few. It is also the responsibility of administrator to keep track of God's "store house"; what's coming in and what's going out.

Some ministries may be offended by this saying: "all of that isn't necessary", but it is! Not only does this establish accountability, but this is also a way to be proactive in battle against the actions of the enemy. When things are not in order, organized, and accounted for, this gives the enemy tools and ammunition to cause unnecessary stumbling blocks and therefore throw off the main focus which is going forth in power and winning souls for Christ.

Remember we are at war, so let's stay armed and dangerous. Keep record of functions such as baptisms, marriages, purchases, tithes and offerings, prophesies, and everything else that the Lord has done and is doing. This shows God that we are faithful and committed.

Just as there are natural administrations, there are also spiritual administrations. A spiritual administration may be an elevation of one of God's faithful servants to the next spiritual call in their life; the award of more power and responsibility (spoken in detail later). One may be elevated or appointed as an Elder or a Bishop in addition to his calling the Lord has given.

Just as these examples are mentioned as positive administrations, there are also demotions as well. Samuel gives examples of this situation to us when he is sent as a messenger of God unto Saul. Another example is given using Samson in Judges 16:20....*and he awoke out of his sleep, and said, I will go out as at other times before and shake myself. And he wist not that the Lord had departed from him.*

Because of the unrighteous actions of some of God's soldiers, even the most elite, they can receive chastisements and demotions for improper execution of orders, and failure to complete assignments. Be obedient to the voice of God, not acting on your own accord. Don't pick and choose what you are willing to do and what you won't do. You are the vessel. Decrease in the flesh and let the Spirit do the work of the Lord, thoroughly and with completion.

OPERATIONS

1 Corinthians 12:6

But there are diversities of operations, but it is the same God which worketh all in all.

From a spiritual military perspective, we, as the church have a responsibility to operate by the Spirit and be in the right place at the right time if we expect to be victorious in battle and render the enemy ineffective. One of the problems within the body of Christ is that many are in the wrong operation or are operating inappropriately and this has allowed for the enemy to gain ground and penetrate many of our lines of defense.

Oftentimes, many have heard the call of God to go into ministry, and with excitement, have answered the call. Of course, by answering the call and being chosen to do a work, the Lord will qualify you for that work which He desires for you to do. However, though many have the same calling, the Lord in many cases doesn't want us to have the same type of operation as others we've seen or may associate with. Of course, the Lord wants us to maintain our Holiness and righteousness; but with so many diverse personalities, cultures, nations, and because the enemy is so crafty, we cannot all operate the same.

Isaiah 43:19

Behold, I will do a new thing; now it shall spring forth; shall ye not know it? I will even make a way in the wilderness, and rivers in the desert.

God is indeed doing a new thing so don't even waste your time thinking He will operate the same in you. For example, if you just answered the call as a pastor; that doesn't mean that God wants you to go out and lease a church building. Look at our natural military. For instance, there are bases everywhere. Is it the will and purpose of Christ for you to even be established in the location where you are right now? Where is the location of your operation going to be established? How does the Lord desire for you to operate? Is this going to be a covert operation or a special operation? What will your role be on the battlefield for Christ? What are the responsibilities that will accompany such an operation? How will this operation be funded, both short and long-term? These are just some of the questions that should be asked when launching a new "base" in the Lord's military.

Many people make the assumption that after getting ordained and accepting their calling that they can succeed by operating like their spiritual mothers and fathers that they have seen become successful. Yes, that is common sense, but that's man's wisdom (wisdom of the world). However, spiritual wisdom prompts us to ask what the Lord wants us to do.

1 Corinthians 12:29

Are all apostles? Are all prophets? Are all teachers? Are all workers of miracles?

I believe the Lord reminds us with such a scripture that all cannot have the same operation of the Spirit. We are many members of one body and must function properly so that the body will experience the overall victory that the Lord desires for us.

If our operation is inoperable or malfunctioning, then we find ourselves out of order. Though this may not be intentional, it is still factual and puts many of us in situations where we may be walking in disobedience. When you're in disobedience you cannot receive all that the Lord has for you to receive. For this reason, many go on a downward spiral; losing hope, faith, and ultimately falling away or getting wounded on the battlefield, rendering them incapable of fighting. In warfare terms, one becomes a POW (prisoner of war), MIA (missing in action), AWOL (Absent without leave), or KIA (killed in action) and in need of revival.

Many of us created or taken hold of habits where we make and implement plans without consulting the Lord first, but simply ask God to bless what we're about to do. When in fact we should get the orders of instruction first, then implement an effective plan of execution, and then ask for the Lord's blessing. Keep the main thing, the main thing. He is our Commander; it's not the other way around. Stick with the full instructions of the operation and mission without adding to or taking away from your objectives and responsibilities. You will gain spiritual ground and be effective in warfare against the enemy's many strategic tactics for destruction.

SPEAKING IN OTHER TONGUES

OTHER TONGUES AND UNKNOWN TONGUES

Speaking in tongues, though it is the evidence of the indwelling, it is the subject of the least discussion. Many have the gift of the Holy Ghost, however, few have the appropriate instruction on how to operate in the Spirit and the appropriate use of such a gift. As with most gifts, there is a correct and incorrect way in which it should or should not be used.

Besides speaking in tongues as our private prayer language with the Lord and for the edification of our spirit, speaking in an unknown tongue is also used to build up or edify the body of Christ. Usually this is experienced amongst a group of believers on one accord.

First, let me mention that speaking in an unknown tongue is different from speaking in other tongues. Speaking in an unknown tongue involves speaking to God in your spiritual language for purposes of edification and receipt of instruction. Sometimes it can be thought of as an information upload and an information download from Christ. This type of communication is for the believer.

However, speaking in other tongues is a sign for the non-believer. Other tongues manifests as several other languages. In the book of Acts chapter two an example is given to us when the people of another dialect heard the disciples speak to them in their native tongue. So, hypothetically speaking, if I have never learned the Spanish language but I began speaking in Spanish because the Holy Ghost has come upon me, then this gift has manifested.

Speaking in tongues must be done in decently and in order. The projection of tongues in the midst of a congregation should be done for the edification of all those that can hear. Once spoken aloud there should be an interpretation to follow and be delivered to that body of people that heard the original tongue projector. Usually there is a Prophet in the midst doing the speaking or giving the confirmation (but not always). If there is no interpretation then that person is out of order and that is not the works of the Holy Ghost (I Cor 14:27-28). Do not project your voice while speaking in tongues unless you are led of the Holy Ghost it is only then that there will be an interpretation. God is not the author of confusion.

RELINQUISHING AUTHORITY

Romans 2:4 reminds us that speaking in tongues is done as the Lord gives utterance. We do not so this for form or fashion. We speak as we are led by the Holy Ghost to speak.

In order to be led of the Spirit you must relinquish all authority and control unto God. This requires complete and total trust in the Most High God. We cannot quench the Spirit and think we are doing things according to the will and purpose of God. I believe that's one of the reasons why Paul stated that he will decrease so that the Spirit may increase (John 3:30).

There is a great bit of confusion, discord, and division among those in the Christian sector. This deals partly with the fact that the Spirit is being quenched and therefore the church is running on personal agendas and endeavors, instead of according to the will of God. For this reason, Paul declares in ICor 1:14 "I thank God that I baptized none of you." Christ is not divided and a Kingdom divided cannot stand. However, where there is unity there is strength.

Some people fail to realize that there is more than one right way to do things and still be obedient to God. We could avoid discord if we could grasp this concept. We can still can the same end result when things aren't done "our way". So let's make sure we are always pressing toward the mark so that we are in a good spiritual position to be used by God.

The Apostles of Old (the originals) weren't building their own kingdom...notice I said their OWN kingdom. They were building the kingdom of God. The religious system that man has put into place MUST be done away with. I've encountered some ministers during my walk who have placed themselves under Bishops or Apostles, surrendering to witchcraft in the Christian sector sometimes with the hope of being exalted by the leadership after a period of humility and obedience.

Situations like these have gone for so long without ministers being held accountable because the ministers that fall victim have a need to personify God, meaning they seek of His flesh instead of His spirit. Even after all of the warnings and biblical stories we've read in the scriptures, many still have a desire for a "king" in the flesh. Because of this we appoint coverings that are not of God, relinquishing our God-given authority, in most cases to people/leadership that are less qualified, less anointed, and have less power. This creates a veil making it hard to hear from the Lord until you restore yourself back to the place you were in him where He is the Head.

Isaiah 30:1

> *Woe to the rebellious children, saith the Lord, that take counsel, but not of me; and take cover with a covering, but not of my Spirit, that they may add sin to sin.*

Oftentimes, we find ourselves doing things to feed the flesh or even because it's what we have seen someone else do, though it may not be the will of God. Sometimes the Lord will give us the desires of our heart even if it contradicts His perfect will for our lives. Don't relinquish our authority because you allow your own will or the will of the flesh to overrule the will of the Spirit.

Remember that the enemy has no power or authority besides what we may give to him. Will you give it to him? Don't surrender your power or authority to the enemy simply because of what your eyes see or because of the situations you are faced with. The enemy will give you a warped presentation of how things really are. So, understand that when you're in spiritual warfare it's not always what you see but that you don't see. You must stand on what and who you know…Christ. Rely on the "intel" you've already been given by the Most High.

I had an acquaintance who was called to be an Apostle. Though He was called to be an Apostle and greatly desired to be what God had called him to be, he didn't particularly care for the responsibilities of such a call. He didn't want to build from the ground. He didn't want to go where no foundation was laid before and he refused to completely surrender and walk by faith. He wanted a ready-made church; to include a building and its members.

One day a Bishop came along who had exactly what he was looking for. This Bishop owned a local church facility and he also had a fairly reasonable numbered flock. However, this Bishop desired to operate a church in another town which was somewhat of a ways away. So the Bishop made the Apostle an "offer he couldn't refuse". He said, "You come under me, run this church as the Lord leads you and as far as the building, send me what you can (monetarily) until you get on your feet."

Does this sound familiar? Man often comes up with his own agenda and leans to his own understanding. Then we simply ask God to bless it. Are we building our own kingdom? Or are we building the kingdom of God? What does the Lord want? Did anyone ask?

If the Apostle is the highest call that there is (to my knowledge), then why cover yourself with a cover? The original Apostles were connected directly with the Most High. Nevertheless, in this situation, the Apostle covered himself (notice I said himself...God didn't do that) with someone of lesser God-given authority unbeknownst to himself. He surrendered his God-given authority to this Bishop and in turn placed himself under a curse. How? The Bishop was a womanizer and was cursed by God even before he made this unauthorized alignment. But he would have known if he would have sought God on the matter. By taking this covering the Apostle created a veil between himself and the Lord. He stopped hearing from the Lord and didn't until he broke ties with the Bishop and humbled himself at the foot of Jesus with sincere repentance. However, before getting to the point of surrender, the Apostle had drained all of his financial resources, lost his home, and an unnecessary strain was placed on his marriage. What he did, though it seemed harmless at the time, was out of order and wasn't lined up with the will and purpose of Christ.

How can preaching the gospel be against the will of Christ? Clearly the Apostle just wanted to preach and be used by God to win souls, right? The operations of the Spirit are diverse. The gifts and talents of this Apostle were not ordained for that ministry that he placed himself over. That wasn't his flock. Can the hand do the work of the foot? Some may say, yes, but with the knowledge and understanding that it would not be with ease or much comfort. The bottom-line was that this was his own will and stemmed from the desire of the flesh.

God does not need us to "help" him work things out for us. Don't allow the enemy to have you rationalize your reasoning for relinquishing your power and authority merely to fulfill the desires of the flesh. Delight yourself in the laws of the Lord and His precepts. The Lord will grant you the desires of your heart, but what price are you willing to pay for those things that don't originate from the will of God? Is it worth the expense of your personal relationship with Christ or your Heavenly reward? Don't allow the enemy to convince you into believing that there is a price to pay for something that in actuality you already OWN (how can he bargain with you for things that already belong to you?) or have been promised by the Most High.

Matthew 4:8

> *Again, the devil taketh Him up into an exceeding high mountain, and sheweth him all the kingdoms of the world, and the glory of them;*
>
> *And saith unto Him, all these things will I give thee, if thou will fall down and worship me.*

All these things Satan tempted Jesus with, even though the scriptures tell us that the earth is the Lord's and the fullness thereof (1 Cor 10:26). All things were created by Him and for Him (Col 1:16). So then, how can Satan give or promise things to Christ that already belonged to Him, since even before the foundations? Know this; that our gifts are unto death and are without repentance. Again, I say that the enemy has no dominion and has no authority unless it's given to him. Know the enemy's intent when he presents himself to you through diverse trials and situations. Continue to fight the good fight of faith and at no time do you put down your armor or relinquish your authority unless it's to the Most High.

GETTING MORE POWER

As you grow in your relationship with Christ, you will develop stronger desires to please the Lord and you will want to do as much for the Lord as you can. You will desire to win souls for Christ and with His power comes the responsibility to work miracles, signs, and wonders in Jesus' name.

Mark 16:17&20

> *And these signs shall follow them that believe; in my name shall they cast out devils; they shall speak with new tongues.*

> *And they went forth and preached everywhere, the Lord working with them, and confirming the Word with signs following.*

Yes, you need the power of Christ to perform the miracles and works that Christ did. Some works will require more power than others. So one may wonder how to get more power. In the preceding scriptures, the Lord tells us that the signs follow them that believe. Therefore, the power is in your belief. Again, the power is in your belief! The more faith you have and the closer you draw near to God, the more you will be able to do regarding operations of the Spirit.

Refer back to the story of the disciples who were approached with a situation of a man whom they could not help. They asked Jesus why they could not cast out the spirits and Jesus answered that some come forth only by fasting and prayer (Mk 9:28-29).

Before the Lord Jesus went forth with His ministry of miracles and works, He prayed and fasted forty days and forty nights. Fasting and prayer increases our closeness to God and puts our flesh under subjection. During this process all doubt about what the Lord is willing to do is removed, and you find yourself on one accord with what the Lord wants you to do. Faith is increased overall and in turn so is your power to operate in the Spirit.

The Spirit of God also desires a Holy vessel to operate within. As you continue to seek the face of God and show yourself loyal and faithful to the instructions God has given, then the Lord will be more inclined to add more responsibilities to your plate. Of course, with more responsibility will also come the necessary power to function and carry out those assigned tasks.

Keep in mind that God is in control. If you don't have enough power to perform certain operations of the Spirit and you have been steady walking in Holiness and righteousness, then God has not ordained that for you to do in that season. God's timing is important. He knows what He is doing and will ordain the appropriate time for all things.

We know that the power of God within us is dependent upon our faith and that the stronger our faith is, the more power we will have to operate. But, does our power have anything to do with our anointing? The two are co-related but they are not exactly the same. The anointing contains power but faith is required to activate such power to heal, deliver, or break yokes. The power of the Holy is a gift and again I remind you that gifts are without repentance. While the anointing of Christ can be taken away and those who are stripped of their anointing will know.

Some are anointed to do diverse things whether it be to sing, to preach, or to play an instrument; the list is infinite. Don't get stripped of your anointing because you've "pimped" it out or used it inappropriately.

When you find that the power you have is seeming to be less effective when in high combat, you may find that you need to break down some more flesh. The Spirit is willing but the flesh is weak. Sometimes we find ourselves in the permissive will of God and outside of His perfect will. We can only do so much in the flesh. To operate as we ought to, we need to be in the Spirit. We must be empty without any residue of ourselves. It is then that we are operating with the full power and authority of God and not on our own power. When the Lord has that empty vessel, it is then that the oil will continue to run and pour and operate through you until you're no longer empty.

To be most effective, one must elevate above the present circumstances or situations. You must elevate above the cares of this world. You must elevate beyond the pictures that the enemy may have painted in front of you. You cannot think logically but you must move in sync with the Holy Ghost.

Don't be so hungry for power that you find yourself willing to take shortcuts. Jesus doesn't want us to hunger after power. He wants us to hunger for his righteousness. Let not your desires be amiss, because the enemy will know and will offer you the ability to fulfill those desires at a very hefty price; your soul.

James 4:2-3

> Ye lust, and have not: and desire to have, and cannot obtain: ye fight and war, yet ye have not, because ye ask not.

> Ask, and receive not, because ye ask amiss, that ye may consume it upon your lusts.

The fact is that there are no shortcuts with Christ. You must go through the Lord's refining process. Sometimes we can confuse a desire of the flesh with that of the Spirit. You must be willing to breakdown flesh to receive what it is you desire from the Lord, especially when it comes to His power.

Beware of the tactics of the enemy. He stands in the midst waiting and even attempting to create and open door for you to walk through. Satan offers to provide what you consider a need but it is temporary. He offers temporary relief and temporary void fillers. He even offers power, but his power is counterfeit and cannot measure up to the Most High. Yes, God is the originator of all power but through Christ He has given us a measure through His indwelling and it is possible to relinquish this power to others even our enemies.

The enemy, too, has been given a measure of power. But know that there is a price for receiving power from the enemy and you must ask yourself if it is really worth it. You will see many operate with the power and authority of the prince of this air and call it Christ. This is why the Lord reminds us that we shall know them by their fruits. Don't sell your soul for a temporary fix. Wait on the Lord and he will strengthen you to go on unto perfection in Him.

There were times when I struggled with the warfare (though I still do). Being that Christ said that we may go boldly to the throne of grace, which is exactly what I did. I laid before God and began to cry out to Him. "Lord, how can you give me all this power and these weapons, but they don't work? What is going on? The power I have is not sufficient," I said. "I need more."

The Lord responded of how disappointed He was for me to even mention such things. He reminded me of how he has re-assured me on numerous occasions that He has fully equipped me and that I was "complete" in Him. The problem wasn't the power, the anointing, or the spiritual weapons, but it was the operator behind the weapons…me.

I had the power of God but I was still clinging to my own authority and control. I still refused to completely surrender all authority to the will of Christ. No. I wasn't practicing sin. I was walking in holiness and righteousness. However, you cannot experience the full manifestation of the power of God with a half-way surrender. I was still hanging onto "self" afraid to completely let the flesh die. There is no way to please God or get any type of victory in the flesh! Even the smallest amount of "residue" of self in the vessel being used by God interferes with the ability to be the most effective in battle.

Don't think or analyze! Prepare the way of the Lord, make His paths straight and He will do the rest. Knowing this, that ultimately the battle is not yours, it's the Lord's.

CHAPTER VI

SPIRITUAL THEN NATURAL

....ON EARTH AS IT IS IN HEAVEN

SPIRITUAL THEN NATURAL

Nothing has manifested in the natural realm that has not first existing in the spiritual realm. This is another reason why our Holy Ghost power is so important. This power is necessary to pull those things from the spiritual real into the natural earthly realm.

BINDING AND LOOSING

Matt 16:19

> And I will give unto thee the keys of the Kingdom of Heaven: and whatsoever thou shalt bind on earth shall be bound in heaven and whatsoever shall be loosed on earth shall be loosed in Heaven.

With our God-given power we have the ability to bind anything and loose anything. Be conscious that you're binding what should be bound and loosing what should be loosed. With such a powerful weapon, we should be so careful to avoid friendly fire.

We want to bind the hands of the enemy in every shape, fashion, form or dimension that he may come. Bind depression, oppression, and suppression. Bind anger, wrath, anxiety, or unforgiveness. Whatever spirits of darkness that may be lurking; bind them up and send them back to the pits of hell.

Some may instruct spirits (because we have this authority) to go back from whence you came. I don't recommend that. If some has been delivered from that spirit you will be instructing that spirit to back to that person, placing them in position to be bound up again. Understand that when spirits are cast out of a person they need some place to go. We have the power and the authority to tell them to go back to the pits of hell.

Be sure to loose things that are necessary for kingdom building and the edification of the saints of God. Loose the fruits of the spirit and gifts such as wisdom, knowledge, and understanding; both spiritual and natural. Loose faith, patience, long suffering, and even diligence to seek the face of God. We can loose the Holy Ghost to rest, rule, and reign.

Keep in mind that whatever is bound or loosed in the natural realm will also be in the spiritual realm. With so great a gift as the Holy Ghost, be mindful of what you are doing. Go forth with boldness and confidence. Build up the Kingdom of God and tear down the walls and strongholds of the enemy.

Remember that warfare never stops regardless of situations or how you feel. We can bind and loose in several ways; on of which is with your mouth. We can speak those things that be not as though they were (Rom 4:17). This works both ways for the positive and negative. So be mindful to maintain self-control even when presented with unpleasant situations that may cause emotions to rise such as anger and disappointment. We are carriers of great power and need not react on emotions or feelings but in power, love, and soundness of mind.

Another way in which we can bind or loose is through our actions and deeds. We operate in faith and faith without works is dead (Jas 2:26). Let our works be before the Lord in the Spirit of excellence without wavering and without compromise. When the works that we do are works of disobedience and rebellion, then these spirits are what we have loosed. Keep in mind that partial obedience is still disobedience.

This should be important to leaders or even parents. When you are the head of a flock, small or large, what you bind and loose has a trickle-down effect and can be transferred to your children or congregation. Be ever so diligent to seek the face of God and die to the flesh so that the Spirit may reign in all aspects of your life.

WATER BAPTISM

Baptism of the Holy Ghost with fire is considered the spiritual baptism. However, the water baptism is still very necessary. The water baptism is a seal of your faith with the water symbolizing the Spirit of God. The water baptism states that not only do you confess with your mouth and believe with you heart but love is an action Word and it shows God with your actions your desire for new life in Him. The Presbytery takes the old man down into the water and the new man emerges; spiritual then natural.

Does one baptism have to come before the other? No! Whether there is a water baptism or you witness some be baptized with the indwelling of the Holy Ghost; both are earthly manifestations with our natural eye and both have already been ordained and existed in Spirit long before being seen on earth.

Rom 8:29-30

> *For whom He did foreknow, He also did predestinate to be conformed to the image of His son, that he might be the first born among many brethren.*
>
> *Moreover whom He did predestinate, them He also called, them He also justified: and whom He justified, them He also glorified.*

I know that we've been commissioned to sow seeds, and even water so that God may grant the increase. I myself have become frustrated on occasion because I didn't see any of the seeds that I had planted yield a harvest. I didn't want much, just something. Then The Lord reminded me of His process. You can plant but the seeds need water too. There is a natural growth process as well as a spiritual process, but both are required.

So before you run off thinking that you have bad seeds or that you haven't sown on good ground, check the water supply. You can't do things half way. God is a thorough God. You need to be sure and ask people if they've ever been baptized. Then, in due season, look for the harvest. Remember what the Lord said:

Matt 28:19-20

> *Go ye therefore, and teach all nations, baptizing them in the name of the Father, and of the Son, and of the Holy Ghost:*
>
> *Teaching them to observe all things whatsoever I have commanded you: and, lo, I am with you always, even unto the end of the world. Amen.*

When we find that we aren't getting results, go back to the Word of God. Be sure you have followed the complete instructions, not adding to or taking away from it. Once you've done all you can do, then stand and see the salvation of the Lord. There is a process and waiting on the Lord is required! Though we all need the spiritual indwelling of the Holy Spirit, let's not neglect to baptize with water. For every spiritual there is, indeed, a natural.

LAYING ON OF HANDS

The gifts of the Spirit are distributed as the Lord wills. However, not always is one born with their gifts. Some gifts come by fasting, prayer, or by laying on of the lands.

We can find examples where the standard was set for this process of gifting or ordination in several books of the Old Testament. One example in particular is when the Prophet Samuel was sent to lay hands and anoint David to be King and to take reign after Saul.

I Tim 4:14

> Neglect not the gift that is in thee, which was given thee by prophesy, with the laying on of the hands by the presbytery.

In obedience to the Lord, oftentimes, the Lord will send a prophet to anoint and lay hands on a being declaring the will of the Lord over their life. This could be a declaration of a gifting, calling, or other words of wisdom, knowledge, or prophesy.

I remember when the Lord sent a prophet to anoint me and declare that God had given me the gift of healing. The prophet also stated "you have healing in your hands, thus saith the Lord, go lay hands upon the sick that they may recover."

Of course, I wanted to be obedient and being still full of zeal, I started to go around visiting local hospitals and nursing homes. After the staff began to see me quite frequently, they advised me that there were certain requirement to be recognized as clergy and to be authorized to see patients that you didn't know. I needed to register with the hospitals and nursing homes and go through the "process" to include showing certification of ordination, consent to a background check, and attend orientation classes.

I was more than willing to oblige but it interrupted my ability to be obedient for well over a week (yes, it's silly looking back on this situation). I went to the Lord and asked why it was so difficult to do what He has instructed me to do.

"What am I supposed to do now?" I asked.

I can't go back there until after the orientation and even then they will I assign me patients to see, I can't just go to whomever I want to.

Then the angel of the Lord as I was praying and stated, "Pastor, laying on of the hands is not just a natural gesture. Everything natural must first be spiritual. Spiritual then natural, my daughter. Lay hands in the Spirit with fasting, praying, and speaking those things that be not into existence. Laying on of hands in the natural sense is merely a confirmation and seal of your faith, for the healing already exists in the spiritual realm."

I said, "Yes, Lord. Now I understand."

So instances when I couldn't always be present to lay hands and pray, I would still lay hands on them in spirit until God opened the doors to be present in the flesh. Keep in mind that if it is the will of God for you or anyone else to be healed, delivered, or whatever the case may be; there is no law , restriction, regulation, or devil that will block or hinder God's will. Remember that the law is not made for the righteous but for the sinner. We as the righteous in Christ are not subject to or bound by the law.

I Tim 1:9

> *Knowing this, that the law is not made for a righteous man, but for the lawless and disobedient, for the ungodly and for sinners, and unholy and profane, for murderers of fathers and murderers of mothers, for manslayers…*

I Tim 5:22

> *Lay hands suddenly on no man, neither be partakes of other man's sins: Keep thyself pure.*

The Lord urges us not to lay hands on any man suddenly. One reason is because of spiritual transference. Understand that spiritual transference takes place through many shapes, fashions, forms and dimensions. So a spirit may move from one person to another; one of those ways is through touch or laying on of the hands.

Let's remind a little. Many people are suppressed, oppressed, and even depressed by demonic forces and are in need of healing or deliverance. One of the reasons why they are in this state is because of two reasons: either it originated from God, or it originated from the devil.

For this reason is the above mentioned scripture broken into two parts. In the first, the Lord tells us not to be hasty to lay hands. Ask yourself why you are laying on hands. Is it to heal? Is it to deliver? Do you have an assignment or mission from God (especially you prophets/prophetess)? Remember we are in the midst of spiritual warfare and we are always dealing not with flesh and blood, but with demonic forces, principalities, and spiritual wickedness in high places.

In most cases, you will witness the presbytery (when being done appropriately) ask a series of questions to the subject prior to laying hands on them. This happens because the two must be on one accord before doing so. Whether being anointed for ministry, desiring to receive the Holy Ghost, desiring healing or deliverance; regardless of the reasoning, the subject should be aware and on one accord with what's going on.

You cannot lay hands to heal a person, or deliver a person that doesn't want to be healed. You'll be wasting your time and your anointing power. Folks that don't want healing or deliverance need to be placed in the hands of the Lord. Pray for them on your own time that they will have a change of heart. Keep in mind that it's not just them that you are dealing with but the demonic forces behind the faces. Don't subject yourself unless you all can agree.

Matt 18:19

> *Again I say unto you, that if two of you shall agree on earth as touching anything that they shall ask, it*

shall be done for them of my father which is in Heaven.

Now there will be some occasions where one will desire to be healed or delivered from something but the thing originated from God. This is where the second part of the scripture comes to play. "Neither be partaker of other men's sins." We don't want to lay hands on someone and interfere with a work that God is doing in someone's life.

I Sam 16:14

But the Spirit of the Lord departed from Saul, and an evil spirit from the Lord troubled him.

In this particular case, a spirit was sent by the Lord because of Saul's disobedience in following God's instructions. It would have been inappropriate if Samuel laid hands on Saul for any reason beyond what God instructed at that point.

I remember a situation I was in a time ago and because of the situation I was experiencing a great bit of doubt about whether the Lord would operate on my behalf. My financial situation was extremely tight, so tight that there was absolutely no room for error with my decision making. Every dollar was calculated and I couldn't afford (literally) to make the wrong decision. I was trying on every avenue to hear the voice of God. I couldn't get it wrong. I was filled with anxiety. Then one day the Lord came to me and stated that I would be struck with sickness. "You will be sick because of your worry. Praise me and I will heal you."

There was nothing that anyone could do for me. There was no shortcut that I could take. Things had to its course. There was no prophet I could call, lest they would take on my sin.

However, on the other hand, some oppressions, depressions, and suppressions as well as other strong holds may come from the enemy over the course of living life and being a mere subject to spiritual warfare. We have the power as well as the authority. The only thing that would hinder us is our faith or lack thereof.

The third and final part of the scripture says: "keeping thyself pure." Laying on of hands is an act of spiritual warfare. When engaging you must put on your whole armor. Part of this armor is the breastplate of righteousness. You must go into war purified of demonic forces and with a repented heart. You place yourself in position to transfer spirits to others and the enemy will use any unrighteousness or sin to his advantage in this fight, managing to distract you or fill you with doubt. There is no such thing as the blind leading the blind. Where is the success in that?

The bible tells us that Jesus is the author and the finisher of our faith (Heb 12:2). Magnifying the word "finisher"; the Lord does not leave any Job undone.

Philippians 1:6

> Being confident of this very thing, that He who hath begun a good work in you will perform it until the day of Jesus Christ.

If this be the case then please understand that when God delivers or heal you, the job is done thoroughly and completely. If He uses you or anyone to lay hands on someone, all demonic forces must vacate that instant. There is no partial healing or deliverance. Whom the son sets free is truly free indeed (John 8:36). Spiritual warfare is a serious matter. Don't play around with demonic forces. Cast them out and wrap things up. Demonic forces always have friends so call them all forth and do a thorough cleansing.

Matt 12:43-45

> When the unclean spirit is gone out of a man, He walketh through dry places, seeking rest, and findeth none.
>
> Then he saith, I will return into my house from whence I came out; and when he come findeth it empty, swept and garnished.
>
> Then goeth he, and taketh with himself seven other spirits more wicked than himself, and they enter in and dwell there: and the last state of that man is worse than the first. Even so shall it be also unto this wicked generation.

See, usually when dealing with situations, no matter what type of bondage they are in, there is almost always more than one spirit in operation. The spirits come and they bring their friends.

There was a time in my life where I was dealing heavily with anxiety which stemmed from shaky faith. With this anxiety came friends named doubt, fear, frustration, agitation, and control. Even if I could eliminate one of the spirits there were others that still lurked and lingered. So recognize what is in operation when laying on hands and casting out devils so that there are none left behind. Again, I say that whom the son sets free is truly free indeed.

CASTING OUT DEVILS

Now, more than ever, the Lord is pouring out His Spirit upon all flesh. Why? Not just because He said He would, but because there is a great need for such a powerful weapon to fight the good fight of faith and to overcome.

There is only one thing worse than not having the power to fight. That is having the power to fight and trample over the enemy but not putting it to use. The Lord came to me on one occasion and said "The enemy is laughing at you right now. You have the power to speak things out of your mouth. The angel that I have given charge over thee cannot move on your behalf because you refuse to speak things out of your mouth. Yes, I know what's on your heart and mind but I will not move until it's spoken." From that point on I've been speaking God's Word back to Him, the enemy, and everyone else who would listen, for that matter. But speaking His Word is only one use of the Holy Ghost.

Mark 16:17

> And these signs will follow them that believe; in my name shall they cast out devils, they shall take up serpents and if they drink any deadly thing; it shall not hurt them; they shall lay hand on the sick, and they shall recover.

Earlier we talked about laying on of hands. After closely watching the standard that Jesus set for us when He walked the earth we find that at no time did Jesus lay hands on one that was possessed with a devil. When He cast out devils there was a command given to come out, and there was a second command given to the demonic force instructed them where to go.

Casting out of devils can fall under the subcategory classification of deliverance. If there is a situation where a healing and deliverance are necessary, then the deliverance should precede the healing process especially where laying on of hands is required.

Binding of spirits and casting out devils are co-related but there is a difference between the two. The difference is that binding and loosing consists of the utilization of the Holy Ghost as a weapon for daily warfare to contend against the enemy as he presents himself in several fashions and dimensions. Whereas that casting out of devils limits the spiritual situation to demonic possession of a vessel.

When casting out demonic forces the same pre-requisite process applies as in the laying on of hands. You need to know the person's state of being. Was the situation from birth? Who did sin, the person or their parents? Are they at the age of accountability? Does God have His hand on them? Keep in mind that God is not a half-way God. Know how many demonic forces you are dealing with and remove them all. Be sure to test by asking the confession of Jesus Christ as the son of God because an anti-Christ will not confess such a thing.

Once you determine the spiritual state of that person that is possessed, you must then be sensitive enough to the Holy Ghost to know if it's God's will for this person to be delivered. Do they even want to be delivered? If the person is not at the age of accountability and they were brought to you by their parents, be sure the parents are saved and have repented unto God.

The longer a person has been possessed with a devil usually determines the amount of faith required for removal. These situations are why the Lord advises us that some things come out only by fasting and prayer. Though all situations require faith.

Mark 9:29

> And He said unto them, this kind can come forth by nothing, but by prayer and fasting.

A quick word of wisdom: don't confuse anointing with power. You can have the double-portion anointing of Elisha and still not be able to cast out a devil. The power is in YOUR belief. The anointing may signify God's presence with you but you control how much you believe that the Lord is able to move in situations. The more you believe, the more power you will have.

Know the spiritual processes that take place in the lives of many before possession occurs. Understand that spirits must be fed. Just like with anything that requires feeding. When you feed it, it grows. Spirits may present themselves in several shapes, fashions, forms and dimensions. It is important to recognize the spirits at work and bind them. The more you continue to "entertain" spirits that lurk and linger or "feed" them, the more they begin to manifest and make a permanent sanctuary or dwelling place.

If you don't pick up your weapons and fight, you will allow yourself to become more and more oppressed by demonic forces. These forces become comfortable enough to bring their friends. Resist the devil and he will flee (Jas 4:7).

DEPRESSION, OPPRESSION, AND SUPPRESSION

There are three other spiritual processes that influence demonic possession. These are depression, oppression, and suppression. Not all are required to take place in order for possession to occur, however, two of the three usually do.

With spirits of depression comes the feeling of hollowing out and emptiness. These spirits also bring along other friends such as hopelessness and suicide. This is an inward feeling of the flesh usually a result of an oppressor or oppression. It is important to be spiritual minded and spiritually sensitive so that you can recognize the immediate presence of such spirits and bind them. Grasp tightly onto your joy and put on the garment of praise to lift spirits of heaviness.

Oppression is the exercise of cruel and unjust punishment by a power, entity, or authority. For this reason it is important not to relinquish your authority to anyone or any being besides the Lord and your spiritual head. When spirits of oppression are present they manifest as heavy weights and extreme burdens that seem nearly impossible to release. Oppression is usually initiated from an outside source. Satan is the chief oppressor, desiring to wear out the saints of God. He knows he can't have your soul (if you're a believer) so he'll attempt to devour the very presence of God within you, making your living situation seam unbearable. He authors the feelings of emptiness, loneliness, and makes one feel God-forsaken.

Suppression is usually the final stage before full possession of a vessel. When a person is suppressed by a demonic force, the person (vessel) and the demonic force start to become one. That person's own will to do things is suppressed or stopped. Their own personality is suppressed and they begin to take on the characteristics of the demonic force. Once this stage approaches, it becomes extremely difficult to fight back on your own. At this level, rarely does anyone see the real you. Though spiritually you are considered in a suppressed state, in the natural sense the doctors of the world dress it up and call it such things as borderline personality disorder, multiple personality disorder, or bi-polar disorder; to name a few.

Once one reaches the state of full blown possession, the demonic force has all authority over the vessel. The demonic force or entity has taken over completely and the host no longer has control over their own actions. This is how a person can become a serial killer or serial rapist, for example, and not have any remorse or even any recollection of events that have occurred.

Devils aren't limited to only possessing vessels, but they can also possess homes, buildings, and even territories. I was subject to such a situation when I purchased my first home several years ago. The home had three levels and the bottom level was the basement. Initially, I didn't bless the house because I wasn't at a high enough level spiritually to grasp such a concept. Once my family got settled into our new home things started to turn sour. Every night it seemed as if there was a spirit of division that came and attacked me. I would want to fight and argue with my husband all night and I didn't get tired. Morning would come and I would still be at it trying to make a stupid point about something without real meaning. Not only did I have feelings of hate, but if I wasn't a Christian, I would have attempted to kill my husband. I went on high speed car chases and the whole-nine.

There was a hate spirit in our house and the sanctuary was the basement. One day as I was away from the house in my office at work I began to pray. It was revealed to me at that time that I had been dealing with a demonic force and that I needed to bless the house with oil. I called over another Christian friend of mine and began to walk through the house placing oil on all of the walls. While I was praying, my discernment led me to the basement. As I drew closer to the demonic force the spirit of fear came over me but I knew I had to complete the process for the sake of my family and the children. I told my friend to read scriptures aloud while I prayed and pleaded the blood of Jesus. The name HATE came into my spirit. Then I commanded in the name of Jesus that the spirit of Hate, you spirit of darkness, come out and return back to the pits of hell. I must admit I wasn't strong in the faith at the time and so the process took about fifteen minutes repeating over and over again until the spirit fled.

In another situation of possession, I allowed an outside guest to come and stay in my house. I considered my house a house of refuge and this person was considered a Christian so as my reasonable service it was a no-brainer. Though I had grown a great deal spiritually, I simply was not prepared for what I was about to encounter. My house had been blessed and had been made a sanctuary for the Most High God. I welcomed this individual in and allowed them to stay in the guest room. The first night was fine and peaceful. On day two I went through my normal day to day routine where I wake up, go into prayer, and enter into praise and worship. Once I got going into a high level of worship, things started to happen. My television cut itself on and then the volume increased on its own. I became distracted as the enemy desired me to be. Needless to say, my prayer ended and I became focused on finding the remote for the TV and at the same time I wondered what on earth happened, while trying to determine if there had been a power surge. Everyone else thought I had lost my mind, but inside I considered the matter.

That night I happened to still be awake while everyone else was sleeping. All of a sudden the air conditioning clicked on. Normally I kept it off and not on automatic but I reasoned within myself that my husband must had touched it earlier. So I went into the hallway and clicked the system off. Two minutes later I heard it click back on again. This time I knew it wasn't me. I wasn't going crazy! My heart began to flutter as reality began to set in and I put all of the pieces together. My guest was the only common denominator in this situation. Then I began to question God under my breath; "Do I fight or don't I? Do I have the authority or don't I?" There was a guest living in my house who was possessed with a demonic force and demon felt the liberty to roam and wreak havoc in my house while the host was sleep. I invited them in. The host vessel was at the age of accountability so my hands were tied with what I could do unless my guest acknowledged the entity and desired to be delivered...but right then they were sleep! Just as I was about to walk into the room and wake them up the demon manifested itself in front of me. It was then that I heard a voice ask, "Do you really want to know?" and the spirit walked into the bathroom. I followed. It stood in front of the mirror and asked "when you look at me, what do you see?" I didn't respond. Then I began to rebuke the spirit, but it wouldn't flee. I finally asked "what is your name? Tell me, what is your name?" It answered, covetousness. I commanded, covetousness, you spirit of darkness, you back to the pits of hell in the name of Jesus. It didn't leave, of course. Things got so loud that my guest eventually woke up and the demon disappeared (from the view of my natural eye). I talked my guest, or who I thought was my guest and asked if she would fight hard enough to be delivered but she said that I didn't know what I was talking about (of course). So I said she had to go. After she left, my husband and I blessed the house again, covered the children with oil and prayed over them, and swept the house of any lurking spirits that may have been left behind.

RULES OF ENGAGEMENT

You've got to know the rules of engagement when casting out devils. This is warfare and there are rules of war. Though we have the power and the authority of the Most High God, we must know and understand where out authority lies. For example, though the U.S. Air Force may have the resources and air power capable to fly into certain territories, there are still certain "no-fly" zones which have been established. This means that if someone enters into these "no-fly" zones, those that have authority over those zones can shoot anyone crossing into these zones and ask questions later.

Be a good steward over the power and authority that God has given you. Do not abuse or misuse it. To avoid unnecessary wounds and trauma; know what authority you have and where to draw the lines of limitation. Know where the enemies' turf is and if you go behind enemy lines, make sure you are authorized by the Most High so that you are covered and spiritual re-enforcements will be sent for you if needed.

So in plain English; don't go picking fights and side battles just because you feel like you have the power to win. Some devils just need to be left alone unless you've been given specific instructions to deal with them. I have asked the Lord "I know have the power, but do I have the authority to handle this? Is this your will, Lord?" Ask, if you're uncertain.

In certain situations of possession, like the about mentioned situation, the person was at the age of accountability and I had to recognize that it was not my power that was lacking but that I lacked the authority because that vessel was a consenting adult. They have to make the choice on their own to be delivered. You cannot decide for them and this is where you have to recognize that darkness and light have no dwelling place together.

I believe for this same reason is why Paul was forbidden to go into Asia and Bithynia by the Holy Spirit. He was not given authorization by God and I believe it was partly due to the great deal of demonic forces they would encounter when they had gotten there. The time was not yet for such a war.

Acts 16:6-7

> Now when they had gone throughout Phrygia and the region of Galatia, and were forbidden of the Holy Ghost to preach the Word in Asia,
>
> After they were come to Mysia, they assayed to go into Bithynia: but the Spirit suffered them not.

ANOINTING OIL

As I mentioned earlier, what's one in the natural is preceded in spirit first. The anointing oil is a natural seal of what's already been set spiritually. The oil symbolizes the Spirit of God.

Lev 8:10

> And Moses took the anointing oil, and anointed the tabernacle and all that was therein and sanctified them.

The anointing oil even dating back to the days of old when God used Moses to set the law and standards for the children of Israel, was used to signify the presence of God with an individual marking them as chosen to higher levels of holiness.

In the above mentioned scripture passage, when taken literally, Moses takes the anointing oil and places it all over the tabernacle and everything inside of it. This symbolized the covering of God and setting aside as a place of holiness.

Now being no longer under the law but under grace, we receive the revelation that we are that tabernacle (our bodies). We are the vessels which house the Spirit of God. We anoint our heads, our homes, and all that therein is as a symbol of God's covering and being set aside unto holiness and righteousness.

With the oil symbolizing the presence of God, I often advise the saints of God to anoint their children daily as well as the walls and things within, especially after the purchase of a new home or other building structure. This is a seal of your faith and states that all that you have you are giving back to God as the keeper.

Anointing oil is used by the prophets and presbyteries for the sake of ordination or the pronunciation of God's will upon someone in the natural realm. Kings of old didn't just become king, but were anointed with oil by renown (respected/recognized) prophets of the Most High and the call was declared over their life.

Saul was sought out by the prophet Samuel and anointed as King. David, too, was sought out as instructed by God and anointed King to reign after Saul. Even though both mentioned kings were anointed early (in their youth) a process still took its course over time before they actually walked in their anointed calling.

Anointing oil not only symbolizes the Spirit of God, but also contains the power of God necessary to assist with anointing, or casting out devils. In order for the oil to contain such power the possessor must fast and pray over it as led by the Lord. You will find that oil has various other uses but no spiritual work can be completed without the power of God and the faith that goes along with every work.

GUARDING YOUR ANOINTING

Just as we have natural strength and energy we also have spiritual strength and energy. It is important to maintain high levels of power, strength, and anointing so that you're always prepared and ready to be used by God when the time comes. One way in which to do this is to guard your anointing.

When our power or anointing levels are low it becomes rather difficult to do the work of the Lord. However, don't be confused. Just because your anointing levels are low doesn't mean you're not anointed or you're anointing "went away". When you're doing the work of God or operating in your gifts or calling; whether it be preaching, praying, laying on of hands. Sometimes signs, healings, and other works are left undone or incomplete, not because of your faith but because you've been drained and you're in need of refueling.

Christ shows us this example when approached by the woman with the issue of blood. She touched the hem of His garment and he responded: "who touched me? I felt virtue leave me." Though he didn't need to refuel because He had undergone such a long fast prior to His ministry starting, oftentimes we do. One may feel virtue leave when in long phone conversations that seem insignificant, or while performing the more obvious operations such as preaching or praying for the sick.

When you find yourself becoming spiritually drained it is necessary to refuel with high praise and praying in the Spirit (your prayer language). Minimize long conversations even though they may seem meaningless or superficial. Also avoid large crowds or places where demonic forces and activity are on high levels such as malls and grocery stores, or concerts and clubs. Don't pray in large "corporate" prayer meetings where there is a great concentration of people on lower spiritual levels that can feed on your anointing (unless you're led by God).

You'll know that you're spiritually drained when no natural thing can fix your fatigue. There is no natural solution for a spiritual problem. Though you get sleep, you're still tired. Though you drink coffee, take all sorts of vitamins, and eat right, you just don't feel 100% yourself. This is when it can be considered a spiritual situation and should be addressed with a spiritual remedy.

CHAPTER VII

BEWARE OF.......

WITCHCRAFT IN THE CHRISTIAN SECTOR

Oftentimes, we as Christian people turn a deaf ear when we hear sayings of the word witchcraft. Sometimes many think it doesn't apply to them or it's not something that they have to worry about. Wrong! A great bit of witchcraft is within the church. I'm sure you've heard the saying "the devil has a seat in the front row", speaking of the church pews on a Sunday morning.

Witchcraft doesn't just originate from old ladies with black attire and broom sticks with dark basements, caldrons, and crystal balls. Witchcraft starts with rebellion. In I Samuel 15:23 it is written "Rebellion is as the sin of witchcraft, and stubbornness as iniquity and idolatry. Because thou hast rejected the Word of the Lord…..Clearly, witchcraft could be defined simply as the rejection of the Word of God. All of us been guilty of this a time or two.

Let's understand that the Word if God comes in several forms. We recognize the biblical form, but it also comes through our leadership whether via apostle, pastors, teachers, or any other lay person. Witchcraft begins to peek its head in the midst of the church when one makes the decision to rebel against leadership and those that God has placed in our midst for guidance and direction.

Oftentimes, you may have witnessed this or even experienced this within the church due to one coming to the conclusion that they have "arrived" because they have been used by God to exercise certain gifts such as the prophetic or healing, to name a few. Though God may be exalting you within the ministry and utilized you within certain "operations" of His Spirit, doesn't mean you give yourself a title and go start your own ministry. Be sure not to get wrapped up in pride, covetousness, and vanity. Let God use you and when the time is right He will do things in decency and in order.

Listen closely; what does that sound like to you? Control and manipulation are two friends that have teamed up in the church to usher in witchcraft. No one really wants to relinquish authority and control to another party. However, it is required to enter into the gates of Heaven. We must surrender totally to the will of God and let our flesh die. Obedience is better than sacrifice. We must trust that God's way is the right way and that those who Sheppard us are doing the right thing. I believe that is one of the reason's that the Apostle Paul says "follow me as I follow Christ" (ICor11:1). Don't assume that people are not following simply because you are not seeing or getting what you want. This is also why we need the Spirit of truth to lead and guide us so that we don't lie to ourselves or begin to rationalize and manipulate in order for things to go in our favor.

The Queen of manipulation, control, and witchcraft was Jezebel. Though Ahab was King, Jezebel was the one that ran everything from behind the scenes. Usually with the spirit of Jezebel in operation you will recognize a person who seems to be a responsible party or one in charge but usually they are merely the vessel being manipulated to work things in the favor of the one functioning behind the scenes. This spirit though sounding feminine, knows no gender, meaning one with a Jezebel spirit can be male or female.

It was Jezebel that issued orders for the prophets of the Most High God to be put to death. It was also Jezebel that manipulated and deceived the Elders and Nobles to move against Naboth so that he would be put to death just so Ahab the King could take over the vineyard (I Kings 21:8).

I can remember being new to pastorship and being requested to speak at a number of services. It never failed that after seeing the anointing that God had placed on my life, various other pastors would try to pull me in several directions wanting me to become a part of the ministry God had given them. It was their desire for me to run diverse programs and be a prominent part of their ministry instead going forth and being obedient to what God had already instructed me to do.

 Please keep in mind that there are several administrations of the Spirit as well as operations. We cannot control people and the gifts that God has given them and think that we are upright in the sight of God. The witchcraft and working of iniquity comes into being when you find that you're not getting the answer you want but you push people or manipulate to maneuver things to going your way anyway.

I can remember telling a few ministers "no, I cannot allow you to demote me to be your assistant, that's not what God told me to do. I will not submit myself under you just for you to re-ordain me as pastor in in two years all for the sake of what you and your people want to do." This is propaganda and not what God wants us to do. After saying no' all sorts of petitions went up to Heaven in desire for my demise. "Working of iniquity" is the sugar-coated version of what took place in the spiritual realm. It was a mess, and a warfare was unleashed that even the "generals of warfare" don't want to face."

It is important that we decrease and have the Spirit of God to increase. This is not about us and what we want. These are not our people; they belong to God. Say "not my will, but thy will be done, Lord."

Eph 4:30

And grieve not the Holy Spirit of God, whereby ye are sealed unto the day of redemption.

We grieve the Holy Spirit when we allow other spirits to come front and center and the Spirit of God is put on the "backburner", so to speak. We must keep the flesh under subjection. It is impossible to please God in the flesh (Rom8:8).

To avoid working iniquity and grieving the Holy Ghost we must not entertain other spirits. Spirits of control, manipulation, jealousy, envy, or anger. Whatever the spirit is, we cannot allow it to operate. When we do, that spirit is more inclined to stay, invite friends, and starts wreaking havoc in our lives.

When we allow this, we continue to be suppressed, oppressed, or depressed with spirits. The spirit of God is a

Spirit of Truth, Holiness, and Righteousness. It is grieved when it cannot freely operate in the vessel it dwells within. Keep in mind, where the Spirit of the Lord is, there is Liberty (2 Cor 3:17).

Because of this, it is important to stay cleansed of spirits or demonic forces. We must ask the Lord to create in us a clean heart and renew a righteous spirit within us. When we are not cleansed of spirits they are more inclined to operate and it becomes easier for you to work iniquity or witchcraft against others within the church and you may not be aware that it is originating from you.

You can't go praying for folk or preaching and ministering without cleansing yourself or sanctifying yourself. The bible says that the Spirit maketh intercession for us with groaning which cannot be uttered (Rom 8:26). If that spirit is not the spirit of God but a spirit that we've been entertaining then, again, I mention that iniquity is initiated in the spirit realm.

In instances like this, one may think they are praying to Jesus but in fact that spirit that is operating in the forefront is making intercession to its own commander among the spirits of darkness. Again, I mention that this is how working of iniquity is initiated in the spiritual realm, whether you're consciously aware or not! Don't grieve the Holy Ghost.

The power of God is just that, powerful! It is our responsibility to make sure we are good stewards over such power. God's power in the wrong hands can be dangerous. There is one who has fallen but who has been highly anointed with the power of God. Keep in mind that gifts are unto death. I say that to say that not all people who have the Holy Spirit will use it properly. The Spirit of God is a weapon and weapons can be misused.

Speaking of weapons; sometimes when we are in positions of power we see others who are also in positions with power. There are instances where you may see operations of the Spirit in which people are healed, delivered, and set free. Other times, you may see signs and wonders. However, some of these similar works will stem from a "spiritual movement". Which is not the divine move of God. It can be hard to recognize those who have fallen and who misuse the power of God. I will reiterate a point made earlier; you will know them by their fruits.

Remember the story of Moses and how he was instructed by God to go to Pharaoh and ask him to let the people of Israel go? Well, there were several occasions when the Lord used Moses and Aaron to show signs and wonders in Egypt. However, the magicians on a few occasions showed the same wonders with their enchantments (see Exodus 8:7). The enemy is very good at mimic and mockery.

In spiritual warfare you will find that there will always be counterfeits and wolves in sheep's clothing. For this reason, the Lord instructs us to know them which labor among you (I Tim 5:12)

I John 2:19

> *They went out from us, but they were not of us; for if they had been of us, they would no doubt have continued with us: but they went out, that they*

might be made manifest that they were not all of us.

So beware of what is God and what is of man .Be careful to avoid being associated with propaganda. It is our responsibility to be sure people see and experience the real thing. We set the standard. Know this also that if it's God then it is not selfish. The Spirit speaks not of itself but speaks that which it sees and hears (John 16:13).

When you take yourself and your agenda out of the equation then you are less likely to get caught up in witchcraft or working of iniquity. Humble yourself under the power and authority of God.

The bible says that whosoever commits sin is a servant of sin. So it would only make sense that if you operate by the Spirit of God then you're a servant of the Spirit.

Colossians 2:18

> *Let no man beguile you of your reward in a voluntary humility and worshipping of angels, intruding into those things which he hath not seen, vainly puffed up by his fleshly mind.*

You can rest assured knowing that if you have the Holy Ghost there will be times where you may be approached by angels. Some will be angels of light and some will be angels of darkness presenting themselves as angels of light. We should believe not every spirit, but try the spirit whether it be of God (I John 4:1).

At no time should one voluntarily humble themselves in the worship of angels whether it be angels of light or darkness. No matter what the reason. Be anxious for nothing; not even for the power of God! Many make extreme sacrifices for such power but the sacrifices are made in vain.

I Cor 10:20

> But I say, that the things which the gentiles sacrifice, they sacrifice to devils, and not to God: and I would not that you should fellowship with devils.

Many people make such sacrifices thinking that the sacrifice is for the greater good. One may sacrifice for money rationalizing that it is needed for ministry, or they may sacrifice for the prestige, or to gain membership. Regardless of the reason, one cannot make sacrifices at the expense of our heavenly reward; eternal life! The wages of sin is death…(Rom 6:23)

II Cor 11:12-15

> But what I do, that will I do, that I may cut off occasion from them which desire occasion; that wherein they glory, they may be found as we.
>
> For such are false apostles, deceitful workers, transforming themselves into the Apostles of Christ.
>
> And no marvel; for satan himself is transformed into an angel of light
>
> Therefore it is no great thing if his ministers also be transformed as the ministers of righteousness; whose end shall be according to the works.

While being a possessor of the gift of the Holy Ghost, you should know that it is a highly sought after weapon of warfare. No solely by those in the natural realm, but most definitely by those fallen ones in the spiritual realm. Just as the Holy Ghost needs willing vessels, so too do demonic forces, principalities, and rulers of darkness. If they can sway you to use your power to their advantage then they will do just that.

Demonic forces manifest is numerous fashions, forms, and dimensions. Be sure to practice "weapon safety" and being careful to avoid friendly fire and even self-inflicted wounds. Your weapons of warfare to include the Holy Ghost should be used by you for the purposes of buildings the Kingdom of God and tearing down the works of satan. We don't want to be categorized as false apostles, false teachers, false prophets or even workers of iniquity. If it's not God, then it's the flesh! With God there is no gray area. You're hot or cold; wicked or Holy; righteous or unrighteous; saved or damned.

Many are spiritually sensitive which is how you want to be for the Holy Ghost to take the lead in your life. Be sure to be sensitive to ONLY the Holy Ghost. Some are just as sensitive to spirits of darkness (others may call them spiritual conduits). Be sure you're on full alert and you stay warfare minded at all times. Stay focused on the mission. Jesus says His sheep know His voice and a stranger they will not follow.

SEDUCING SPIRITS AND DOCTRINES OF DEMONS

To seduce someone would be to persuade them to do or perform an activity or deed that may be forbidden or inadvisable and may be something that they would never do voluntarily through their own will.

1 Tim 4:1

> Now the Spirit speaketh expressly, that in the latter times some shall depart from the faith, giving heed to seducing spirits, and doctrines of devils;

During this era, many have fallen away and have departed from the faith. Numerous demonic forces and spirits of darkness have been released from the pits of hell. The enemy desires to sift us like wheat. He will use any means necessary to do it.

Some also have fallen away and taken hold to a doctrine of a demon. An example of a doctrine of a demon is when people may preach parts of the Bible but may say such things like there is no hell, or that hell is on earth. They may suggest that some parts of the scripture should not be taken literally. These folks should be left alone to be accursed.

Galatians 1:6-8

> I marvel that ye are so soon removed from Him that called you into the grace of Christ unto another gospel:

Which is not another; but there be some that trouble you, and would pervert the gospel of Christ.

But though we, or an angel from Heaven, preach any other gospel unto you than that which we have preached unto you let him be accursed.

God is the ancient of days. He is the same yesterday, today, and forever and changes not. When you hear or are presented with some information that conflicts with the Word which you have already be taught, then believe it not. Don't hesitate or rationalize ways in which it could be true. The beautiful thing about the Holy Ghost is that it is the Spirit of Truth. I f something is not right then the Holy Ghost will make it known unto you.

Many fall into the trap of the enemy and believe doctrines of demons because of unanswered questions and a burning desire for sensible answers. Some questions can be answered with the Word of God. Some answers will be revealed over time as you grow and continue to seek the face of God. However, some things we must understand will never be made known.

Seducing spirits come along to take advantage of the fact that you're grasping for answers relentlessly. A prominent I know fell because of this. He could not deal with the fact that his family members that he loved strongly could have gone to hell because of their lifestyle. Based on what is written in the Word of God his loved ones had an eternal home in hell. He became plagued with that devastating information and couldn't get closure with such a notion. To put his soul at ease the enemy convinced him that there was no hell and that's what he began to preach. So in the end, he will be joining his friends and family in hell and all of this started because of spiritual questions that he didn't like the answers to and seducing spirits.

Don't base decisions on feelings. The Holy Spirit doesn't operate on emotions or how difficult it may be to process the truth. The truth is what it is and we cannot be responsible for decisions that others choose to make about their salvation.

REVEALING OF SECRETS

There is a spiritual movement where the false apostles, false prophets, and false teachers have gone from place to place speaking of secret revelations claiming that such revelations have been given to only them by God. Please understand that there is nothing new under the sun. The Lord warned us of such a time in His Word.

Luke 8:10

> *And He said, unto you it is given to know the mysteries of the Kingdom of God: but to others in parables; that seeing they might not see, and hearing they might not understand.*

Luke 12:2

> *For there is nothing covered that shall not be revealed; neither hid that shall not be known.*

There is no such thing as a secret revelation. Through the Spirit of God (Holy Ghost), all things are made known to us. Jesus doesn't single one being out. Jesus IS the revelation!

God makes know His mysteries to us by His Spirit and through His prophets. The Lord is pouring out His Spirit upon all flesh, so those claiming to have secret revelations of information from on high should be rebuked.

God is the revealer of secrets. As Paul shares with us in his letter to the Galatians that false brethren unawares are brought in to spy out our liberties in Christ that they might also bring us into bondage again (Gal 2:4). We must allow the Spirit of Truth to be sovereign. No longer can we remain silent! The time has come and now is, that we expose the enemy in our camps and wherever else he may be. We are the undertakers of the enemy. He must be stopped and put to flight!

THE IMAGE

Gen 1:26

And God said, let us make man in our image, after our likeness:.....

Before we were yet formed in the womb it was the desire of God to make us in His image and likeness. It is such a privilege for He has favored us and made us even higher than the angels. To add to such a privilege, He has blessed us with his Power and authority...and the devil is NOT happy about it.

Since the beginning after his fall from Heaven, satan has found the need to mock and mimic the privileges given to us by God. He desires to duplicate our image in order to gain access to our lines of defense hoping to further his ultimate mission which is to kill, steal, and destroy. Even as we mentioned in earlier chapters that he presents himself as an angel of light to deceive and seduce the children of God.

2 Corinthians 3:18

> *But we all, with open face beholding as in a glass the glory of the Lord, are changed into the same image from glory to glory, as even by the Spirit of the Lord.*

There was one night I was taken to a place by an angel of the Lord. Whether in a dream or vision, I know not. But what I beheld was a mirror seemingly transparent, yet not. And as I looked on I beheld a demon without a face dressed in an all-black cloak. The faceless demon walked back and forth behind the mirror. Then I saw people whom I knew not. They began walking in front of the mirror, and behold, a voice I heard saying, "come let me show you how it is done. Do you really want to know?" It was then that I saw the demon transfer from the spiritual realm into the natural realm attaching itself to the person in the mirror. These things I had seen astonished me, but in my heart I considered the matter.

The Lord allowed this vision to be a revelation on one of the many ways and dimensions the enemy uses to transfer from the spiritual realm and manifest itself in the natural. Think about what an image is, just that, a picture. We should be presenting an image of God to those around us. Don't allow the enemy to distort the picture of God in you. You must love what you see. If you don't, the enemy will use it to create doubt and wreak havoc in your life. The image of God that you portray to others should have them desire the REAL thing, the original. As you know when it comes to paintings and portraits, the original is always worth so much more. Don't allow the enemy to create a duplicate image of you and use it to build his kingdom instead.

POINT OF NO RETURN

Hebrews 6:4

> *For it is impossible for those who were once enlightened; and have tasted of the heavenly gift and were made partakers of the Holy Ghost.*

> *And have tasted the good Word of God, and the powers of the world to come.*

> *If they shall fall away , to renew them again unto repentance, seeing they crucify to themselves the son of God afresh, and put him to an open shame.*

I've heard of a saying "once saved, always saved." This is not a true saying and there is proof in the Word of God. Do not be deceived. Many have started humbly with the gift of the Holy Ghost and over time have convinced themselves that they can turn to the things of this world and still enter into the kingdom of God.

My bible asks the question: "shall we sin, that grace may abound? God forbid" (Rom 6:1-2). Please get a full understanding. As children of God we do not practice sin and willingly and knowingly turn back to the world that had us bound in the beginning. Backsliding is one thing, but a complete falling away is an entirely different matter altogether.

People who have been enlightened by the Holy Ghost can't knowingly go worship the devil, indulge in sorcery, divination, or other wickedness; simply repent and return back to God. The Holy Ghost will convict you even when your heart comes up with the idea to put forth such actions of disobedience and rebellion. However, once you go through that door, there is no pathway back to the true light.

Because of this very thing God stated in His Word that many will cry out Lord, Lord, I have healed in your name and cast out devils in your name and He shall say to them: "depart from me you workers of iniquity, I knew not of you."

It is not hard to get to that point of no return and for this reason the Lord tells us to put on the whole armor of God that way we may be able to withstand the whiles of the enemy. We must build up our Most Holy faith and be not deceived by seducing spirits and doctrines of devils. Stay prayed up and fasted up. Study to show thyself approved, knowing the Word of God for ourselves and not just trusting what the Pastors or teachers say.

Christian Atheism is another thing to watch out for. When we say with our mouths that we are followers and believers of Christ but our lifestyle reflects that Christ doesn't exist. This pattern of behavior is wrapped in hypocrisy and leaves one encompassed about with all sorts of oppressing spirits and strongholds that will become too powerful for one to overcome on their own. This is a deadly lifestyle to live because the problem is that when travelling down this road, consciously you think you're spiritually fine and one begins to rationalize and justify reasons for practicing sin and doesn't comprehend that they are in need of deliverance. So let's not turn a deaf ear to the conviction of the Holy Ghost because there will be a return of the spirits that were once swept away and the last state of that man will be worse than the first.

FEAR AND INTIMIDATION

PS 56:4&11

In God will I praise His Word, in God I have put my trust; I will not fear what flesh can do unto me.

In God have I put my trust: I will not be afraid of what man can do unto me.

To be most effective in the Spirit we cannot have fear and doubt or allow the enemy to intimidate. We must be complete in Christ.

I JOHN 4:18

There is no fear in love; but perfect love casteth out fear: because fear hath torment. He that feareth is not made perfect in love.

To be complete in Christ we must cast out all fear. The Spirit of God is not effective when you operate in fear and doubt. In order for healing to take place and for deliverance to take place we must allow complete reign of the Holy Spirit.

One of the enemy's number one attacks is fear, intimidation, and distractions. When you're scared you're not using your God-given power in His fullest capacity and when you're distracted you're most likely not using Him at all.

Let's not allow the enemy to gain ground because He has intimidated us. We must put full and complete trust in Christ without wavering and without compromise.

There is lots of work that could get done but that hasn't because of fear. We should not fear what man can do unto us but use perfect purified love to cast out all fear. Christians shouldn't be on the run when they have the power of the Holy Spirit. They should be the ones putting the enemy to flight.

When you have the Holy Spirit There is an increase of spiritual warfare. Most people want to talk about the flowery stuff like miracles, signs, and wonders but they don't want to talk in detail about the warfare associated with such acts of God. You will encounter demonic forces and you must be effective in the Spirit to fight a good fight. The warfare is real. We cannot fear the demonic forces or the encounters they bring. They smell the fear and intimidation and will continue to linger so long as you refuse to operate under the power and authority given by the Holy Spirit. Don't be intimidated into not using your power. Go forth in boldness and confidence.

Miracles, signs, and wonders don't take place without spiritual warfare. In order for miracles to take place there is war in the Spirit. In order for healings and deliverance to take place there is war in the Spirit. Demons must be moved and cast out. You cannot do it in fear. Remember there is nothing that can separate you from the love of Christ.

LUKE 12:4-5

> And I say unto you my friends, be not afraid of them that kill the body, and after that have no more they can do.
>
> But I will forewarn you whom you shall fear: fear Him, which after He hath killed hath power to cast into hell; yea, I say unto you, fear Him.

The Lord desires us to have a healthy, reverent fear of Him as one would have for their Father. The Lord is not a bully. He chastens the ones He loves in hopes of them doing and being better, abounding greatly in faith and love from glory to glory.

Don't be distracted by some things you see. Believe the report of the Lord. Measure it with the Word of the Lord. Put on the whole armor daily and do not entertain those things which are contrary to what the Lord has spoken regarding His children.

Have you ever looked at how someone else was living and became discouraged? Don't allow someone else's lifestyle to dictate your Christian walk. Remember the same God that had patience and longsuffering with you is the same God to have patience and longsuffering with them. Take what would normally be a distraction and use it for encouragement. When you see others becoming distracted, encourage them to stay the course and go the extra mile. That's what the Spirit is for. Pray for them. Fellowship one with another in the Spirit strengthening one another. However, don't allow the enemy to gain ground with tactics of fear, distractions, or discouragement. The race is given to those who pace themselves. Keep running. Let the Spirit of God be your guide and your motivation.

One of the ways I often demonstrated fear was by hesitating and second guessing myself. I would question whether what I was doing was right. However, if we acknowledge the Lord in all of our ways then we know that He will direct our paths. With a mind stayed on Him, seeking holiness and righteousness you won't be steered wrong. Remember that you are not the one doing anything regardless of the spiritual work you are commissioned to do. Whether you're moved to pray, heal, or deliver, the work is done by the Spirit of the Most High. There's no fear when you allow the Spirit to do the work but if you're giving the flesh credit then you're justified for having fear. Man can do nothing. There is no glorying in the flesh. All glory belongs to the Most High.

THE TEARING DOWN

I wasn't a pastor yet...at least the Lord hadn't made mention of it. I was a mortgage broker. I loved helping people and I love math, so doing mortgages put the two into one, helping people get into homes and accounting seemed to be the best of both worlds (it was also very lucrative). Though it may not have seemed that way at first glance, I wasn't a people person. I didn't carry a bubbly, outgoing, or charming personality. I've always been shy, reserved, and somewhat standoffish. Because of this, the Lord has been the driving force making things work behind the scenes and I was content. Most of the work that I did was by telephone with little interaction and most clients rarely saw me until closing.

Because of my passion for patient and nursing care I also signed a contract with the U.S. Air Force Reserves. This would fulfill my desires for emergency medicine practice which I would be obligated to once a month, allowing me to maintain balance doing the things I loved (math as well as science), without getting burned out and overwhelmed.

One day I had reached a tipping point. I was co-owner of a mortgage business headed to military training. Financially things were going well but it was a front for what was really going on emotionally and spiritually.

I was in a bad relationship. It was a relationship that started all wrong. It started on a lie...a lie that I told. I led the fellow to believe that I was a certain age that I was not. So the initial foundation was not built with trust. I didn't trust that He would want me if He knew and He didn't trust me once He eventually found out. The relationship was one of comfort and convenience. We settled. However, I wasn't happy...I wasn't being fulfilled. Something was missing.

This was a relationship of chase. Though He was my natural husband at the time, He wasn't spiritually ordained for me. I chased him for years hoping we would get past the lie I told but it didn't happen. I thought that I did everything I could to get the man to love me but the love wasn't there.

So back to that day.... The tipping point. I was a believer. I went to church often. I prayed prayers (though they were selfish) and I sought the Lord. I loved helping people but I hated myself. I thought I wasn't good enough. One night I finally broke down and cried out to the Lord with my whole heart. "What's wrong with me?" I cried. "What's wrong with me, Lord?"

For the first time in my life I received a response from the Lord. It was prophetic in nature. "Nothing is wrong with you." The Lord replied. He went on to tell me the things I was dealing with spiritually and that I needed to surrender completely and seek Him more. I allotted time to read my word and study daily. He, in the meantime blessed me with a new relationship that He ordained. We would study the word together, pray together, praise and worship together and seek the Lord together. Jesus being the Chief Cornerstone, this was a foundation and relationship built (for success) to last forever.

I soon went off to military training. What I initially thought was a natural wound up having more spiritual revelation than I anticipated. I left somewhat naïve but returned home more spiritually aware and more rooted and grounded than ever before.

I immediately got back to work catching up on a lot of things that lacked while I was gone. Spiritually I grew leaps and bounds but naturally my world came "tumbling down". Suddenly the "successful" mortgage company had business which started to dwindle, loans weren't closing. Employees had to be laid off (let go) and eventually we were out of business. The home we were blessed with had gone to "short sale" and we needed to move! I was seeking the Lord, acknowledging Him in all of my ways...yet that question came to mind again. "What am I doing wrong?" I thought. The Lord told me I was in a season of tearing down. He used those exact words but I thought it was because I had done wrong in the past and though He had forgiven me, I needed to pay the consequences for my actions. Times weren't easy but there was comfort because my Father told me what was going on and that He was allowing it to happen.

In the midst of this tearing down, the Lord kept giving me the unction to speak His word. I was excited about the things the Lord was doing in my life. In the natural sense I was homeless for a while staying in hotels and sometimes with a relative. However, I was seeking the face of God and He was daily making Himself known to me more and more. The insecurities that I had about someone loving me began to dwindle because Jesus loved me and began to show me the depths of His love which couldn't be matched by the world. It was pure. It was complete. Nights I'd wake up with laughter and praise uncontrollably. It was a joy that cannot be described or explained.

One day the Lord told me that He had a ministry for me. The lord told me I was a pastor and that I'd get my start from the radio. He said that I'd lay hands on the sick and they'd recover. I was excited but I must admit that what I saw with my natural eye and what He told me were two different things.

I wasn't a preacher. I wasn't born into a lineage of ministers. I had no natural friends or spiritual friends to go to. I didn't have the personality for it. There was no flock to see with the natural eye. This is a weighty call and I didn't really like people enough.

However, I was obedient and started doing radio broadcasts live every day. Meanwhile, we were hiding our vehicle form the repo man and hoping for a miracle to pay it. I was skilled and yet I couldn't get a job anywhere. To top it off I had a new born baby to care for. The Lord really does have a sense of humor. Every week we had yard sales in hopes that we would sell enough to cover radio expenses, hotel, and diapers.

Family members thought I was crazy. They though I did something wrong. They thought my husband was a dead beat because I was in such a situation. This new faith walk was somewhat overwhelming but I had to trust and put my faith into action leading by example. I already had two strikes against me to start with being that I was a woman and I was young.

The fifteen minute broadcasts that we did weren't a great "profound" word as some would hope, but I spoke the Truth and I shared my testimony. It seemed as if there wasn't anyone who understood or could relate. People who heard our broadcasts didn't call for prayer requests or praise reports. There didn't seem to be a natural support system but the Lord was with us and all I had was faith and obedience. I knew things would get better.

We found a small space for rent that I wanted so that we could hold worship service. At the time I thought it was the right thing to do. I advertised on the radio. I printed flyers and brochures. No one showed up for services, so we preached to the walls until that final day we had to clear out our things because we couldn't pay for the building any longer. I was a pastor of the Most High, but with all of the circumstances and situations it didn't seem like it at all. Most nights I cried out to the Lord while somehow gathering the strength to praise Him. I learned that He was my refuge and my strong tower. I soon found out the difference between knowing something and having the actual experience for yourself.

One late night I finally managed to fall asleep. An angel came unto me and suddenly I had the urge to write. I wrote and I wrote. I couldn't stop writing. All day and all night I wrote for two weeks straight. This birthed template for the book "Pick Up Your Weapons and Fight!" I went from writing to typing as all of my experiences along with the Word of God started to come together and the Lord's purposes for my life started to make sense. I continued to write and speak the Word even though it seemed that no one cared to hear it, especially coming from me.

The Lord led my husband, Demetrius and I, to fellowship with different ministries. I learned more and more about humility and about what takes place behind the scenes. I wasn't religious. I wasn't traditional... I didn't want to be. Something about me was different. I didn't want the same ol', same ol' service. I really wanted to help change peoples' lives I wanted the true restoration. I wanted complete healing and deliverance to take place. I wanted miracles, signs, and wonders to transform and renew the Lord's people. I wanted the true pouring of the Spirit. I wanted people to see what I saw. I wanted them to encounter what I encountered...His Holy Spirit...His power...His depth...His love. How could I make these desires a reality? How could I implement and show forth so great a love? Was anyone listening? There's so much passion but where do you put it when it begins to overflow? It was like "fire shut up in my bones".

The churches my husband and I attempted to fellowship with didn't particularly care for us too much. They said I was out of order. They also mentioned I wasn't a pastor because I was a woman. There was a great bit of pressure to join ministries and have them "cover me", as if man could cover anything. We quickly moved on brushing the "dust" off our feet in those places we weren't wanted. Because I was in my hometown I knew we really didn't have a chance of being really accepted so we decided to be obedient to the Lord's nudge and start fresh in Alabama. We determined to start again while still maintaining the radio broadcast as the Lord instructed us to do.

I knew we needed to make a move but I must admit that the last place that I thought of was Alabama. It wasn't in our thoughts or plans at all. Nonetheless, my husband and prophet advised that it was where the Lord wanted us and so in obedience we went.

The churches and the people seemed to be the same. I wanted to compel men and women to come to Christ, but I was encountered with religion instead of God-fearing reverence and heart-felt desire for more. I grew discouraged and my desire for the task at hand began to dwindle. I didn't want this job! Where was the drawing? Was there anyone the Lord would use me to save? It was a lonely walk. The zeal that I thought I had begun to diminish. Then in the midst of it all, the Lord said that our tearing down was over and to go forth and build. Build what? I didn't want to do it. I wasn't the right one for the job and I was upfront willing to admit it.

There was so much that needed to be done and there was so much that I desired to do for the Lord. I was overwhelmed by the great need to establish a spiritual foundation in others where Jesus was the Chief Cornerstone, but I didn't know where to start. Who was listening? I was obedient but sometimes the spiritual works that I did lacked the joy that the Lord desired for me to have. I told myself over and over that we plant and others may water, but God grants the increase. That's what kept me going searching for that one.

During this tearing down I learned to see people in Christ's eyes. I no longer looked at them at face value but I saw works in progress by a master potter...like trees planted by the rivers of water. I saw possibility!

The Finish

Jesus is a finisher.

Hebrews 12:2&6

> *Looking unto Jesus the author and finisher of our faith;*
> *who for the joy that was set before Him endured the cross,*
> *despising the shame, and is set down at the right hand of*
> *the throne of God.*

> *For whom the Lord loves He chasteneth, and scourgeth*
> *every son whom he receiveth.*

Jesus has set the standard of endurance when He died on the cross. He loved not His life unto the death. Nevertheless, through obedience He carried out the will of God.

He is our source, our joy, and the author of our peace.

II Corinthians 2:20

> *For all the promises of God in Him are yea, and in Him*
> *amen, unto the glory of God by us.*

> *Now He which stablisheth us with you in Christ, and Hath*
> *anointed us is God,*

> *Who hath also sealed us, and given the earnest of the*
> *spirit in our hearts.*

There is no shame in serving Christ. But as I mentioned earlier service requires obedience and endurance. This is easier said than done. Nevertheless, we know that we operate not in our own strength or authority but according to the will and authority of Christ. Remember, the work has already been finished on the cross. We don't pay for Christ has already paid for with His blood. However, we hear the words of the Lord and His instructions and by His Holy Spirit of promise we are led to fulfill his works in obedience.

Hebrews 5:8

> *Though He were a son, yet learned He obedience by the things which He suffered;*
>
> *And being made perfect, He became the author of eternal salvation unto all them that obey Him;*

So we see how important obedience is. Obedience is better than sacrifice. All of the hope of redemption and eternal salvation rests in our willingness to obey.

II Corinthians 8:11-12

> *Now therefore perform the doing of it; that as there was a readiness to will, so there may be a performance also out of that which ye have.*
>
> *For if there first be a willing mind, it is accepted according to that a man hath, and not according to that he hath not.*

We must get a clear understanding of the will and purpose of Christ in our lives. There is one overall vision which is the redemption and reconciliation of souls back to Christ. We all play a role in the fulfillment of that vision and purpose.

I Corinthians 7:20-24

> *Let every man abide in the same calling wherein He was called.*
>
> *Art thou called being a servant? Care not for it: but if thou mayest be made free, use it rather for He that is called in the Lord, being a servant, is the Lord's freeman; likewise also He that is called, being free is Christ's servant.*
>
> *Ye are bought with a price; be ye not the servants of men.*

Brethren, let every man, wherein He is called, therein abide with God.

Know what your purpose is. Jesus asked the question, "Can you drink from this cup?" We must know what's in the cup to partake. When we say to Christ, we are saying yes to being complete in Him and allowing Him to have complete reign that His will can be accomplished through us.

When the servants and the prophets of old set the standards for the people of God as they were commissioned, they were not left hanging to make up things as they went along but the Lord told them of their mission and their purpose. Moses was told to lead the people to the Promised Land and how to do it. Noah was told to build the ark and instructed of its measurements. Jesus instructed His disciples and apostles on the building of the Kingdom, healing of sickness, mending of broken hearts, setting captives free, and all around being lovers and encouragers of one another in the faith.

Romans 12:4

For as we have many members in one body, and all members have not the same office. So we, being many, are one body in Christ, and everyone members one of another.

Romans 12:12

For as the body is one, and hath many members, and all the members of that one body, being many, are one body: so also is Christ.

For by one Spirit are we all baptized into one body, whether we be Jews or Gentiles, whether we be bond or free; and have been all made to drink into one Spirit.

So with this understanding we recognize that all of us have a role to play within the body of Christ. With there being diversities of gifts and roles we know that we don't all have the same office but as one body we are in unity to do operations which allow for the whole body to operate and function accordingly as the Lord has ordained.

We must have a close enough relationship and have effective communication so that we abide wherein we are called and we can do our job thoroughly to completion.

The Lord doesn't want us to be divided in the body. The Spirit of God is not divided. However, sometimes members suffer and when one suffers we all suffer. However, in unity we bear the infirmities of the weak, and pray in the Spirit for those that are in need.

Romans 15:1

> We then that are strong ought to bear the infirmities of the weak and not to please ourselves.
>
> Let every one of us please his neighbor for his good edification.
>
> For even Christ pleased not Himself; but as it is written, the reproaches of them that reproached them fell on me.
>
> For whatsoever things were written for our learning that we would have patience and comfort of the scriptures might have hope.

So the things which we do in the operation of the body must edify Christ. We with one mind and one mouth must glorify God. It is not meant for us to be on the foundation of others for a long period of time but through prayer and supplication they bear our infirmities. We bear the infirmities of each other as helpers of one another.

As members of the body of Christ we must first learn to be servants and as servants before we can serve each other we must be completely given over to Christ.

I Corinthians 8:1

> *Moreover, bretheren, we do you to wit of the grace of God bestowed on the churches of Macedonia; how that in a great trial of affliction the abundance of their joy and their deep poverty abounded unto the riches of their liberality.*

> *For to their power, I bear record, yea, and beyond their power they were willing of themselves; praying us with much entreaty that we would receive the gift, and take upon us the fellowship of the ministering of the saints.*

> *And this they did not as we hoped, but first gave their own selves to the Lord, and unto us by the will of God.*

With the grace that we've been given through Christ we learn that before we are servants even to one another, Christ wants us to be given completely to Him. How can we know what the needs of the saints are and how to minister unto the needs of the saints if we are not first given over to Christ? Only by His Spirit can we search the depths and understand how He desires to pour out His Spirit upon His people.

We spend time at the feet of Christ understanding our identity in Him so that we know as being likeminded and made in His likeness how to meet the needs of others and encourage others to go the extra mile in Christ for the sake of our liberality.

We as members of the body ought to do and go beyond our power with willingness to pray with earnestness that we abound in the love and the faith of Christ receiving the gifts of the Holy Spirit and fellowship one with another.

Effective communication is a key factor in being a servant in the body of Christ. How can one pray earnestly without knowing the need? We don't get the revelation in the Spirit if things aren't made known in the Spirit.

Made in the USA
Columbia, SC
30 October 2023